Abdul Hannan
Hasan M. Mohsin

Are Natural Resources a Curse or Blessing?

GW00632729

Abdul Hannan
Hasan M. Mohsin

Are Natural Resources a Curse or Blessing?

LAP LAMBERT Academic Publishing

Impressum / Imprint

Bibliografische Information der Deutschen Nationalbibliothek: Die Deutsche Nationalbibliothek verzeichnet diese Publikation in der Deutschen Nationalbibliografie; detaillierte bibliografische Daten sind im Internet über http://dnb.d-nb.de abrufbar.
Alle in diesem Buch genannten Marken und Produktnamen unterliegen warenzeichen-, marken- oder patentrechtlichem Schutz bzw. sind Warenzeichen oder eingetragene Warenzeichen der jeweiligen Inhaber. Die Wiedergabe von Marken, Produktnamen, Gebrauchsnamen, Handelsnamen, Warenbezeichnungen u.s.w. in diesem Werk berechtigt auch ohne besondere Kennzeichnung nicht zu der Annahme, dass solche Namen im Sinne der Warenzeichen- und Markenschutzgesetzgebung als frei zu betrachten wären und daher von jedermann benutzt werden dürften.

Bibliographic information published by the Deutsche Nationalbibliothek: The Deutsche Nationalbibliothek lists this publication in the Deutsche Nationalbibliografie; detailed bibliographic data are available in the Internet at http://dnb.d-nb.de.
Any brand names and product names mentioned in this book are subject to trademark, brand or patent protection and are trademarks or registered trademarks of their respective holders. The use of brand names, product names, common names, trade names, product descriptions etc. even without a particular marking in this work is in no way to be construed to mean that such names may be regarded as unrestricted in respect of trademark and brand protection legislation and could thus be used by anyone.

Coverbild / Cover image: www.ingimage.com

Verlag / Publisher:
LAP LAMBERT Academic Publishing
ist ein Imprint der / is a trademark of
OmniScriptum GmbH & Co. KG
Heinrich-Böcking-Str. 6-8, 66121 Saarbrücken, Deutschland / Germany
Email: info@lap-publishing.com

Herstellung: siehe letzte Seite /
Printed at: see last page
ISBN: 978-3-659-34105-2

Dedication

This work is dedicated to my beloved parents, brothers and sisters for their unconditional support during my studies.

Table of Contents

Acknowledgment

First and Foremost, I would like to thank Almighty Allah for being my strength and guide in writing of this thesis. Without Him, I would not have had the wisdom or the physical ability to do so.

I express my gratitude to my supervisor, Dr. Hasan M. Mohsin for his support, valuable comments, and unwavering guidance throughout the course of this work. His special interest and knowledge enabled me the right guidance and provided me much needed motivation.

I am also very thankful to all my class fellows. When times were tough, they gave me the confidence and strength to keep pressing on to achieve all my goals. God bless them all. I appreciate the feedback offered by Mr. Shazad Mehmood, Mr. Salman Ahmed, Mr. Mohammad Ahsan Iqbal, Yasir Khan, Mr. Kamran, Mr. Mohsin Kiyani and Mr. Adeel Khalid.

Finally, I thank everyone in my family for always being supportive of my education, especially my Father and Mother who have all contributed to and encouraged me during my studies.

List of Tables and Figures

CHAPTER 1

Introduction

Natural resources are considered as one of the important components of national wealth and contribute directly to income, employment and fiscal revenues of economies. There are two core types of natural resources on the basis of its regeneration. First, renewable resources that can be restocked by natural process e.g. water resources land, and forests. Second, non-renewable resources that cannot be regenerated e.g. oil and minerals etc.

Importance of natural resources cannot be denied particularly for developing countries as goods produced from various types of natural resources are the backbone of these economies. It can be judged by the fact that natural resources provide 30 % of the total wealth in low income countries which is double from the upper middle income countries while it is only 2 % of total wealth of high income countries [1] (World Bank, 2006). In developing countries share of primary products in production, export and income is often found relatively higher than the industrialized countries thus it is plausible to state that soil and water resources can play a vital role in agriculture sector of low income countries.[2]

Economies that are based on natural resources often provide a better employment and income opportunity to their natives. In this regard it is noteworthy that income of 40 to 60 million people is associated to forestry in one or another way (World Bank, 2004a), moreover 22 to 25 million people are employed in mining and finally 47 million people having a job opportunity in fishery sector [Food and Agriculture Organization of the United Nations (2007)]. Above mentioned statistics depict that almost all types of natural resources can play a crucial role in sustaining long run economic growth of a country.

Management of natural resources is a real challenge for the developing economies due to following reasons. Firstly, it can lead to a long run economic growth, if a country invests some reasonable amount of its earnings from natural capital into human, social and financial capital. Secondly, major portion of export in most of the developing countries consist of primary goods due to their agrarian basis and a frequent change into the prices of these

---

[1] Only OECD countries
[2] Agriculture sectors of developing countries contribute 30% to GDP, while it is 4% in high income countries. (OECD 2007)

primary products often create a trouble in growth of developing countries [Grill Yang, (1988)].

Empirical results provided by ample cross-sectional studies surprisingly report a negative relationship between natural resource abundance and economic growth after controlling the main determinants of economic growth [Auty and Miskesll (1998), Sachs and Warner (1995, 2001),]. However some of the naming researchers called this negative relationship as a conceptual puzzle [Gelb (1988), Auty (1994 and 2001)]. Empirical literature depicts some mixed results which create confusion in deciding, either the natural resource abundance is a blessing or curse.

In this regard advocates of resource curse provide various explanations and claim that, in-effective policies regarding to export and wealth creation by some government can turn the blessing of natural resources into a curse. Government of resource rich countries often ignore the wealth creation activities and rely more on the exports of primary products which delays the competitive industrialization. This delay in competitive industrialization can cause a slow development of labor intensive manufactured exports which generates a low skilled labor and as a result there is a surplus of labor supply particularly in rural areas and a high income inequality boosts up the social strains in society. In order to control social tension and unemployment, governments start to deploy rent of its natural resources to foster the industrialization. Government supports to protect the industrial sector by the rents coming from farm and mines often prove useless when there is a stress and frustration in society. Thus inefficient allocation of resources by the government destroys the investment opportunities in primary sector and as a result resource rich countries locked in staple trap (Auty, 2002). Above mentioned detail discussion provide sound grounds to state that a general belief of considering the resource abundance as a blessing is not satisfactory all the times while effective government policies for export and efficient allocation of resources play a crucial role in long run growth of resource rich countries.

Since resource abundance economies have to face the challenges like Dutch Disease, volatility of export prices of natural resources; rent seeking behavior, thus they needs an appropriate management of natural resources for long run growth . If a boom in natural resources negatively affects the manufacturing or agriculture sector of some economy then this phenomenon is said to be Dutch disease (or in a broader sense Resource Curse). It is noteworthy that there are examples of countries like Mexico, Venezuela, and oil rich Gulf

2

States which failed to grow with rich natural resources, while the countries like Singapore, Hong Kong, Taiwan and South Korea are not rich in natural resources but enjoying higher standard of living. Empirical results of Neary and Van (1986) also confirm the resource curse hypothesis. Above stated examples along with references of international literature reveal that resource curse hypothesis is difficult to deny. However countries relying more on its natural resources may not perform well but some countries using its resources wisely have achieved a rapid growth. For instance, Norway invested its resource revenue on societal trust fund and protected its economy from the Dutch disease. Human capital can plays an important role in avoiding resource curse if rents coming from natural resource are invested in human capital or development projects. Finally it can be stated that efficient use, equitably and sustainability of natural resource can ensure a long run economic growth [Gylfason (2001), Polterovich (2007), Brunnschweiler (2008)].

On the other hand resource deprived countries have strong incentive to develop public goods by promoting efficient investment. Earlier stage of competitive labor-intensive industrialization enhances the rate of urbanization and ensures the sustainability of a rapid economic growth in resource poor countries. South Korea, Hong Kong and Mauritius have experienced the same above mentioned phenomena in their economic growth [Auty (2003)].

Some of the empirical studies also report that natural resource abundance can also affect the economic growth through education and institutions. and Tornell (1996, 1998), Halvar et al (2006); Lane empirically proved that sound institutions can mitigate effect of resource curse by developing institutional framework and rules related to possession of natural resources. Moreover governance plays a key role in management of natural resources. It can be argued that high rent form natural resource may induce political elites to block technological and institutional development as such institution may reduce their power and rents from natural resource. Unclear property right, multiple claims and functions may create monopolies to resources. As a result only a small group benefits from natural resources instead of a country [Acemoglu and Robinson (2006)].

Contrary a sound literature related to resource abundance and economic growth found no evidence of resource curse as some countries experienced high economic growth with abundance of natural resources. Empirical findings of Alexeev and Conrad (2009) suggest that oil and mineral wealth have positive impact on per capita income. Iimi (2006) also concluded that, mature political elite of Botswana got a path of developmental by making an

3

investment in human capital. Advocate of resource blessing school strongly favor those policies which are related to investment in human capital, redistribution of income and growth enhancing activities because these are less likely that resource curse occurs [Snyder et al (2005)].

Diverse literature have used a proxy 'exports of primary product as percentage of GDP' to measure the resource abundance but according to some of the researchers like Brunnschweiler et al (2008) it is not suitable to use this proxy because it measures the resource dependence rather the resource abundance. Moreover, Cavalcanti et al (2011) commented on the methodology which most of the studies follow to explain the impact of natural resource abundance on growth of an economy. He reported that most of the empirical literature relies on cross-sectional approach which does not take into account the time dimension and the problem of specification and endogeniety. Above mentioned detail discussion regarding to methodology and proxies used in empirical literature so for indicates, still a space is available to explore the relationship between natural resource abundance and growth for some economies in more comprehensive way.

The core intention of current study is to investigate the evidence of resource curse in different regions by using proxy of total natural rent as natural resource variable. More explicitly study will concentrate on exploring either the relationship between natural resource and economic growth stands same across various regions, income group and religions i.e. South Asia, East Asia and Pacific, Europe and Central Asia, Middle East and North Africa, Sub Saharan Africa, Latin America and Caribbean, North America and finally in Muslims and Non-Muslims countries. Secondly, study will focus on possible channel through which resource abundance can affect the growth of a country. Finally current study will see how the relationship changes when there is a decomposition of total natural resource rent into oil, gas and mineral rent.

For this purpose current study intends to use a panel data set of 170 countries from the year 1990 to 2010 for a regression analysis. It is noteworthy that regional dummies are also included in estimation process to check either the resource curse belongs to a specific region or not this reduced the sample up to top 40 oil reserve countries.

The significance of current study can be judge by the fact that, among the country level literature of resource curse current study lies in the line of those rare studies which have used such a large sample to have investigations on resource curse hypothesis. Latter half of this study is arranged as under; second chapter will describe the Natural resource Distribution Economic Indicator, third chapter will explain detailed literature on resource curse, and chapter four will enlighten the methodology both theoretically and empirically. Finally results are interpreted in the fifth chapter of this study and conclusion is drawn after discussion of results.

CHAPTER 2

Natural Resource Distribution and Economic Indicators

2.1 Introduction

This chapter provides an overview of distribution of the natural resource regarding to different income group and regional level of countries. There is a comparison of economic indicator of seven regions to discuss the relationship between natural resource and economic growth.

2.2 Comparison of natural capital and other types of wealth by different Income Group

A Comparison of natural capital and other types of wealth by different income group is given below in the following table;

Table 2.1

	1995					2005				
	Total Wealth (US$ billions)	Per Capita Wealth (US$)	In-tangible Capital (%)	Produced Capital (%)	Natural Capital (%)	Total Wealth (US$ billions)	Per Capita Wealth (US$)	In-tangible Capital (%)	Produced Capital (%)	Natural Capital (%)
Low Income	2,447	5,290	48	12	41	3,597	6,138	57	13	30
Low Middle Income	33,950	11,330	45	21	34	58,023	16,903	51	24	25
Upper middle income	36,794	73,540	68	17	15	47,183	81,354	69	16	15
High income OECD	421,641	478,445	80	18	2	551,964	588,315	81	17	2
World	504,548	103,311	76	18	6	673,593	120,475	77	18	5

Source: World Bank estimates

During the year 1995 to 2005 per capita global wealth (in US dollars) has increased and it has grown faster particularly in the low middle-income countries (almost 50% growth in per capita wealth). Initially low middle-income countries were more dependent on the natural resources but during the above mentioned decade, these countries have a change in composition of its natural resources. Statistical detail in above table depicts that these countries have a change for intangible capital (45% to 51%), for natural resource (34% to 25 %) and finally for produced capital[3] it is 21% to 24%. It is noteworthy that natural capital is the sum of nonrenewable resources[4], cropland, pastureland, forested areas[5], and protected areas. In this regard it is also plausible to state that these countries have used natural capital to develop in-tangible and produced assets [Gylfason (2001)].

High income countries hold 82% of world income while low income countries hold less than 1% although having 10% of global population. Intangible asset is the fastest growing in all income countries that is why it has the largest share in total wealth. Some of the naming researchers called this rapid growth as a result of enhancing human capital and improvement in institutions [Gylfason (2001) Subramanian (2003), Isham et al (2005) and (Martin et al (2006),].

2.3 Regional Comparison of Natural Resource

A regional Comparison of natural resources during 1995-2005 is given below into the following   graph;

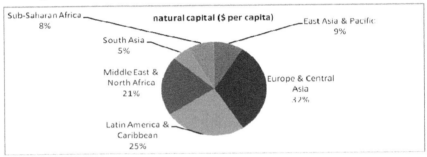

Figure 2.1

The above mentioned graph shows that (Europe & Central Asia), (Latin America & Caribbean) and (Middle East & North America) have higher share of natural capital[6] as compare to the rest of the world. Europe and Central Asian countries have 32 % of World natural capital. Latin America & Caribbean region is blessed with 25 % natural capital of the world. South Asian countries are relatively poor than other part of the world as they have only 5% share in Natural Capital of world. Above statistical detail helps us to conclude that

---

[3] Produced capital is the sum of machinery, equipment, and structures (including infrastructure).
[4] It includes oil, natural gas, coal, and mineral resources
[5] It includes areas used for timber extraction and non-timber forest products.
[6] $ per capita

natural resource are not equally distributed differently that can lead to predict that, the relationship between natural resource and economic may be able to differ across the regions.

2.4 Economic situation at different region of the world

To explain the economic situation of different regions of the world current study has used following statistical details into the table given below,

Table 2.2

Indicator	South Asia	Middle East and North Africa	North America	East Asia and Pacific	Sub Saharan Africa	Europe and Central Asia	Latin America and Caribbean
GDP (constant US$)	$1.52 trillion	$1.8 trillion	$14.2 trillion	$12.3 trillion	$830.4 billion	$17.1 trillion	$3.3 trillion
Population, total	1.6 billion	380.6 million	343.5 million	2.2 million	863.8 million	891.6 million	595 million
Education[7]	88	91	102.94	99.0	69.3	98.3	101.6
GDP per capita, (constant 2005 US$)	$945.2	$4703.7	$41339.4	$5599.1	$961.3	$19160.5	$5586.9
Gross capital formation (% of GDP)	33.6	24.1	15.4	28.1	21.2	18.9	21.7

Source: World Bank data, 2010

Current study has got information that South Asia as one of the poorest region in the world having a low GDP as compare to other regions (i.e. having per capita income equal to $945.2). Report of Multidimensional poverty index by United Nation revealed that 55 percent of people in south Asia and 64.5 percent of people in sub Saharan Africa are MPI-poor. Moreover the World Bank (2005) reported that above 40 percent of the populations in South Asia was living below the international poverty line. Contribution of South Asia in the global income is only 7 percent but its share in global poverty is 43 percent although having one-fifth of the world population. In spite of having natural resources poor economic conditions in South Asia can be reported as a result of poor governance as South Asia has ranked lowest in governance index [See the governance stability index report by Country Risk Guide (ICRG data)].

---

[7] Primary completion rate, total (% of relevant age group)

8

Study has also got information that although Sub-Saharan Africa is rich in natural resource[8] but 50% of its population is living below the international poverty line [World Bank (2005)], it has the lowest GDP along with the lowest education level as compare to rest of regions. Regarding to this contradiction it can be stated that this region is over dependent on agriculture sector that can be judged by the fact that agriculture sector contributes 20% to 30% in its GDP, 50% in its exports (Cotton, coffee, tea, cocoa, sugar, tobacco, major crops) and it employs 60% to 90% of its labor force[9] in this sector. Poor statistics regarding to literacy rate also allow claiming that there is a less investment in human capital in this region and it can be a possible reason of above mentioned contradiction.

Contrary to Sub-Saharan Africa, North American region and East Asia & Pacific region are performing well. North America has highest GDP per capita along with highest level of literacy rate. This region is also well structured in three economic areas i.e. North American Free Trade Agreement(NAFTA) , Central American Common Market(CAMC), Caribbean Community and Common Market (CCCM). As well as East Asia and Pacific have highest per capita income than other regions of the world, growing at the rate of 7.5% which is higher than other region of the world and contributing 40% of global wealth (World Bank, 2012). Economic management enabled East Asia and Pacific to remain resilient and sustain growth[10]. The above mentioned discussion regarding to Sub-Saharan Africa, North American region and East Asia and Pacific regions compel me to state that Governance plays important role in the development and growth of a country. International Country Risk Guide has measured the governance stability index for many countries and according to this report Middle East and North America region have higher governance stability than rest of the world (ICRG data) while South Asia has ranked lowest in governance index.

2.5 Conclusion

Above mentioned discussion reveals us that countries having investment in human capital, less dependent on agriculture sector, good governance and a proper change in decomposition/management of natural resources can enjoy a sustainable economic growth otherwise there can be prevalence of resource curse hypothesis. It is not the only the natural

---

8 Sub-Saharan Africa is one of the major exporters of gold as this region is producing 30% of world's gold and 49 % of world diamond. A major part of new oil reserves are in this region. Moreover Sub-Saharan Africa region is also a major exporters of uranium, chrome, vanadium, antimony, Colton, bauxite, iron ore, copper and manganese.

9 http://worlddefensereview.com

10 http://www.worldbank.org/en/news/feature/2013/04/15/east-asia-pacific-economic-update-april-2013-a-fine-balance

resource which determines the long term growth but other factors also very important for sustain economic growth.

CHAPTER 3

Literature Review

3.1 Introduction

This section is divided into two sub-sections; theoretical literature and empirical literature. Section I, theoretical literature, will give historical and theoretical background of resource curse and factors behind resource curse. It also will describe the relationship between trade and natural resources and an overview of what would be the optimal extraction rate of natural resource. Finally section II provides detailed review of empirical literature on resource curse along with possible channels described by the different authors.

3.2 Theoretical Literature

Different theoretical approaches have been discussed in literature. Gelb (1988) explained the effect of natural resource on economic growth with the help of four different theories i.e. the linkage theory, the neoclassical theory and related growth, export instability theories and booming sector and Dutch disease theory.

Linkage theory has three sub linkages; production, consumption and fiscal linkages. These linkages explain the interaction between the leading and other sector. In Production linkages, intermediate goods accounts smaller portion of final value than other products so these linkages are less important for high rent seeking activities. Consumption linkages may have a favorable or adverse impact on development. Fiscal linkages are very important for high rent seeking activities because resource rent goes directly to the hand of government and most of the time these rents are consumed inefficiently either by the private or public sector. It is also possible that the rent goes to hand small group of policy maker which is likely to decrease efficiency. So it does not stimulate growth.

Neoclassical growth model says resources have a positive impact on growth when rents are used in economic activities like payments of imports of important factor of production. The export instability theory is related to the positive and negative impact of resource income. When resource revenues are used for investment especially public investment then it will have a positive impact on growth. In contrast when saving and investment fall with income, this will have an adverse impact on growth.

Booming sector theory is explained by two effects. One is spending effect and other is resource movement effect. Neary et al (1986) developed a framework by proposing two essential components of Dutch disease theory. Spending effect theory states that discovery of natural resource lead to high domestic income and high expenditure both on traded and none trade goods. Impact of this high income on traded good prices will be very little as these prices are determined in the international market but the prices of non-traded goods will increase as these are determined in the domestic market. Thus profit in the non-trade surge and this high profit attract the investors due to which traded sector shrinks. The second component of Dutch disease is explained by the resource movement effect. It says that boom in the natural resource will increase the marginal productivity of the factors of production which lead to higher prices of factors of production. Some producers will not be able to pay the higher prices to factor of production. Consequently, the traded goods sector start to decline. This effect occurs when labor is required for the natural resource because there are some natural resources which require little or no labor to extract the resources.

Auty (1993) developed a theory on resource curse with the help of linkage and booming sector theories. Study found that resource richness is injurious to those countries which are in early stages of development process. Study also suggested that resource rich countries performed worse than resource poor countries because of mining sector production function as mining sector is highly capital intensive and employs only small fraction of labor force. Most of the machineries or capitals in developing countries were imported from other countries which results in less opportunity for local production linkages to develop local factories.

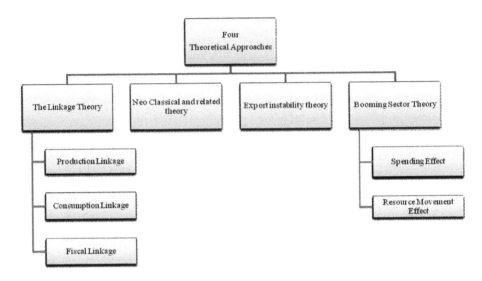

Figure 3.1

Auty (2003) debated that mismanagement of natural resource is the failure of macro-economic policy. Superior performance of resource poor country is due to the pattern of structural change in resource poor countries and delayed development of industrialization in resource abundant countries. Coherent and prudent polices with the aim to increase the social welfare helped the resource poor countries to grow faster than the resource rich counties. Study revealed that resource poor countries adopted those policies that promoted the competitive industrialization while high rents of natural resource in the resource abundant countries fostered factional and predatory political states that promoted sectional interest instead of coherent economic policies. The early start of industrialization enhanced the urbanization, fostered saving, investment and labor intensive manufacturing. In contrast, resource rich countries were more dependent on commodity export which delayed the process of industrialization. Economic diversification is also a major challenge for resource rich countries as these countries were skewed to only few product. Delayed industrialization and slow progress of urbanization created the labor surplus in the rural market that generates the income inequality and social tension. Then government intervened in industrialization process by creating the capital intensive infant industries which took decades to mature. Such

13

industries create a few jobs due to its capital intensive nature; in response government employed additional people to reduce the social tension thus inefficiency prevailed. Study concluded that in 1960s, domestic economic policies to promote the infant industries were one of the main reasons of slow economic progress.

Matsuyama (1992) explained resource curse by developing a model of two sectors i.e. agriculture and manufacturing sector. Study argued that agriculture production will have negative impact on economic growth as agriculture sector employed the major portion of labor force that otherwise would be in manufacturing sector. Study also concluded that this approach is useful when studying labor intensive production of natural resource but nor relevant or less related to natural resource sector such as oil. If there are some externalities or there are some backward and forward linkages then the shrinkage in the manufacturing sector will decline the growth. David Rudd (1996), used the component of Neary et al (1986) and empirically tested the Dutch disease in the Netherlands, Indonesia, Nigeria and found that Dutch disease decline the traditional tradable good sector.

Sachs and Warner, (1995) explained this phenomena with the help of trade and non-trade sector and argued that a massive increase in the natural resource will cause a rise in a country revenue and an appreciation of real exchange rate. High real exchange rate makes the domestic goods relatively expensive and creates low demand for tradable goods. Profit of the exporters fall and production starts to decline as there will be few buyers in the international market. Consequently, the tradable good sector contracts.

Heckscher-Ohlin model (1955) has explained trade theory in the context of natural resources which states that a country with abundance of natural resource will specialize in that particular sector or good. Welfare gain will be achieved because specialization leads to efficient use of resource. Lewis et al (1982) explained that extraction will not lead to over extraction because it is assumed that the extraction is done either by social planner or competitive producer to maximize the welfare of both present and future generation. This holds true when it is assumed that market are perfect and firms are producing under constant return to scale

Sometimes, countries with abundant resources face some challenges which can lead to distortion in the market. Dasgupta et al (1979) explained that natural resource market faces monopolistic structure in which there is only one dominant player and imperfect market

14

structure produces inefficient results. Sometimes cartels of natural resource will behave like a full monopoly and monopolists set prices at level above marginal cost. In this case optimal price and extraction is described by modified Hotelling arbitrage condition which states that optimal price and extraction will be set at which marginal revenue will grow at the rate of interest rate. Lewis et al (1982), explained that depletion of natural resource in this case depends upon depends upon the elasticity of demand. Resource depletion will take place at slow rate when demand elasticity rises with price and it will be higher rate when demand elasticity decreases and depletion will be at same rate when elasticity of demand is constant. Monopoly cartel will preserve the resources longer by controlling the extraction and charging high prices. This shows that monopoly cartel depletes natural resources slower than a perfectly competitive industry. Above theory assumed that both producer and consumer set their extraction path and demand path in light of each other's strategic choice at the beginning of the period.

Brander et al (1997) emphasized the importance of property rights in trade of natural resource and argued that unclear property rights can create a conflict. Open access to particular natural resource will lead to over exploitation and eventually it exhausts the natural resource. Property right is also very important because it define the pattern of trade between two countries. Suppose two countries have same amount of natural resource with same technology and identical taste but have different property rights. In one country the stock of capital is perfectly control but other country have open access to natural resource. It can be said that 2nd country will harvest more than 1st county. If there is open trade then 2nd country will export natural resource to the first country. A Country with weak property rights could also be the exporter to the relatively resource abundant country. Brander and Taylor(1997) also argued that demand of natural plays an important role in trade. Study showed that if demand is relatively high then a country with weak institution could be importer of natural resource rather than exporter. Gylfason (2000) revealed that resource rich countries, especially transition economies, are more dependent on export earnings and prices of primary goods are more volatile thus creating more economic instability in countries. Efficiency would be low as these countries rely heavily on agriculture sector and less scope of manufacturing, trade and services. Another argument about resource curse is that sometimes natural resource abundance gives a false sense of security, which results in misallocation of resource. In contrast, countries with lower natural resources are more careful and feel no margin of errors. Suppose when resource rich countries find itself in a difficult situation and try to encourage growth, then they start borrowing from the foreigners to invest in the domestic projects in order to increase the growth. This results in inflation and debt grows out of control. Eventually country stuck in stagflation or end up with low level of the living standard and public dissatisfaction.

Arezki et al (2007, 2010) emphasized the importance of geographical location as more concentrated resource could lead to conflict which hampers the economic development. In other words, limited supply of natural resource can lead to rent seeking activities. Mostly natural resource sector also faces high return to scale due to high fixed cost of extraction and transportation faced by the resource based companies.

3.4 Empirical literature on Resource Curse Hypothesis:

A comprehensive literature regarding to resource curse is available now but the first wide-ranging empirical attempt was made by Sachs and Warner (1995) which captured the attention of economists. This study identified the negative relationship between economic growth and resource abundance along with explaining the forward and backward linkages as the reason of resource curse. He is also of the view that demand for the manufacturing goods grow higher than demand for primary goods which leads to higher prices for the manufacturing products. By using Openness, investment, quality of bureaucracy and terms of trade index, as independent variables in the regression model they examined the relationship between natural resource exports[11] as a percentage of GDP and per capita annual growth rate by using a cross country analysis. Their empirical findings by using different measures purposed that resource abundance leads to higher rent-seeking and corruption, directly through investment thus lead to slow economic growth.

In 1997, Sachs Warner tested the resource curse using different sample data and found that negative relationship between natural resource abundance[12] and growth. Their results show that natural resource exports tend to lower growth rates during 1971-1989. These results are based on a simple theoretical model of endogenous.

In 1999, Sachs and Warner again investigated the question that if specialization in natural resource is a viable strategy. They used the data of Latin America from 1970 to 1990. By using the model of big push where the transition from cottage industrial to factory production

---

[11] In resource export they include agriculture, mineral and fuels.
[12] Sachs and Warner used the definition of resource abundance as "Exports of primary goods".

plays a vital role along with data of data of Latin America from 1970 to 1990, estimation results indicated negative relationship between resource abundance and growth and after controlling the additional variable the relationship remained negative. The first proxy variable is exported of primary agriculture and basics metals and minerals. The alternate definition includes only basic metals and minerals but relationship remained negative. This paper provided the explanation of Dutch disease and how its transmission affects other variables adversely. Sachs and Warner (2001) expanded their earlier work. According to them geography was missing variable in their earlier work and performed cross country regression to test whether this affects the results or not? The results remained the same as was in their previous study (1995).

Herbertsson et al (2000) examined the Dutch disease in Iceland and empirically tested three symptoms of Dutch disease; the appreciation of real exchange rate caused low level of secondary-sector employment and output, volatility of primary sector leads to volatility of real exchange rate and high investment threshold, wages of primary and secondary sector move together and affects employment and output. Their results showed a positive relationship between primary exports and secondary sector output and negative relationship in the long run. Study showed that when output and wages of primary sector increase then real exchange depreciated thus Dutch disease appeared through the labor market.

Gylfason (2000) found a negative correlation between genuine saving in 1997 and labor share of agriculture in 1990 in sample of transition economies. Variables used in the paper are; corruption and genuine saving, inflation, economic growth and labor force in agriculture. Positive correlation between genuine saving rates and per capita growth is found. Study also used inflation distortion/ implicit rate of inflation tax as a measure of policy failure and found positive relationship with proxy variable of natural resource abundance. Average per capita economic growth in 1990-1997 is significant and negatively correlated with average inflation distortion.

Stijins (2001) examined the relationship between natural resource abundance and economic growth by using the actual data of natural resource and argued that Sachs et al (1995) results are not robust when we change the proxy of natural resource abundance. Author took the data of land area to population from FAOs production yearbook and coal, oil, gas production and reserve data from US Department of Energy (1999). Empirical findings of OLS suggested that natural resource abundance has no significant impact on economic growth when study

17

used actual data of fuel and mineral reserves, and land was negatively correlated with all control variables. Results also indicated that school attendance, aggregate saving and investment rate were positive correlated to all types of reserves. Moreover it was argued that human capital and rule of law in a country encourage the discoveries of oil, gas and mineral; however Dutch disease found in case of land, oil and gas.

Cavalcanti et al (2011) developed theoretical model which is consistent to econometric model and showed long run relationship between natural resource and economic growth. Study argued that previous studies of resource curse did not take into account of time effect and used non-stationary panel methodology by using real data of natural resource, oil production, rent and reserves of 53 oil exporting and importing countries. Empirical findings of the this study showed that there is a positive relationship between natural resource abundance and economic growth and suggested that oil abundance itself is not curse rather welfare enhancing policies and institutions could play a better role in economic growth.

A few studies have argued that low level of human capital is main reason of resource curse. Gylfason (2000) argued in transition economies which mainly depend on the agriculture sector do not need educated people if it is compared by industrial economies where demand for educated people are high. Empirical results suggest that school enrollment at all levels is negatively related to natural resource abundance and positively related to growth.

Bravo-Ortega et al (2005), suggested that negative effect of resource abundance on economic growth is due to shift of resource to natural resource sector from the sectors that could generate faster economic growth. Study argued that resource curse could be eliminated by accumulating natural capital. Empirical analysis of the study showed that human capital has a positive impact on return from natural resource sector.

Lederman et al (2008) used cross-sectional and panel data to test the resource curse hypothesis using different measures of resource abundance. Cross-sectional results indicated that Leamer measure (net natural exports) is positively correlated and become significant after controlling other variables. Resource export variable was negatively correlated with economic growth but the panel data estimations showed this relationship positive and significant. They also suggested that human capital could be an important channel.

Institutions and institutional reforms have played an important role for growth and development. Various studies suggest that countries where institutions are weak, natural resource abundance lower the growth of an economy [Bulte et al (2005), Arezki et al (2007)]. Countries where institutions are producer friendly, resource abundance did not cause lower growth [Halvar et al (2002, 2006)]. Resource abundance surges the level of corruption in countries where democratic institutions are weak, but the same results does not hold in counties where democratic institutions are strong [(Bhattacharyya et al 2009)]. Higher income and better institutions improves development indicators like Human Development Index, the percentage of the population that is undernourished, the percentage of children that are underweight, Human Poverty Index and life expectancy. (Bulte et al 2003).

Arezki et al (2007) described different channels which can affect growth performance. Decline in the non-resource export sector resulted Dutch disease problem and low institutional quality is main reason of resource curse. Study incorporated the an interaction term with institutional quality and with de jure openness in regression model and argued that trade policy can make resource curse less severe. Author used the instruments for the institutional quality, openness and found no evidence of resource curse and Income per capita was explained by the institutions, geography, and de facto openness. After controlling geography, institutions and openness, resource export effect become significant and negative. Study found no evidence for the interaction term of natural resource with Rule of law or openness.

Halvar et al. (2006) used the sample of 87 countries and took primary exports share in GNP as measure resource abundance. Their results indicated that the countries where institutions are producer friendly, resource abundance did not cause lower growth.

Boschini et al (2007) used four different measures of natural resource; primary exports share in GNP, share exports of metals and ores in GNP, mineral production's share in GNP, and value of production of gold, exports of ores and metals, silver and diamonds as a share of GDP. Study has taken the data of 84 countries from Minerals Yearbook, Production data and U.S. Geological Survey (1999). Proxies used to measure institutional quality are; average of indexes for the quality of the bureaucracy, corruption in government, rule of law, the risk of expropriation of private investment and repudiation of contracts by the government, For all different measures, the interaction term came out to be positive and outweighs the negative effect and this effect is highly significant.

Brunnschweiler et al (2008) used new measure of natural resource wealth which is different from Sachs and Warner (1999). Because resource variable is more unstable and author gave the examples of wealthy countries which has low primary export. They added institutional quality variable in growth regression. They found no correlation between Resource export variable and other resource wealth (fuel and nonfuel mineral production developed by World Mineral Statistic; 1978, natural gas taken from British Petroleum). They also use rule of law and government effectiveness as indicator of institutional quality. Results of both OLS and 2SLS method suggest that there is a positive relationship between resource abundance and growth when they used new measure of resource abundance and role of institutions was also considered.

Polterovich et al (2010) have used different indicators for resource abundance such as share of fuel exports, average ratio of net export of fuel to total import, production of oil and gas per capita in 1980 to 1999, proven reserves of oil and gas per capita in 1980 to 1999 and sub soil assets per capita in $US in 1994. For institutional quality they have used various indices such as corruption index 1980 to 1985[13] and investment climate index[14]. They found high correlation between reserve and production. Study found that resource abundance helped to balance the budget, to stabilize price and effected the investment in GDP positively. Regression results indicated that resource export counties have less income inequality and resource export and production has negative impact on the quality of institutional after controlling per capita GDP Results indicated that positive relationship between all indicator of resource abundance and economic growth. It is also suggested by the author that Dutch disease found in those countries where institutions are weak Low domestic fuel prices effect growth positively via increase in competition and negatively via energy waste but first effect pre dominates.

Carmignani et al (2010) has used subsoil assets as resource abundance and institutional quality is measured by one minus ration of currency in circulation to M2. He took the data of 65 countries for the period of 1980-2005 and used 2SLS method. Results indicated that resource abundance increases the inequality which leads to low level of human development. It is also found that good Institutions have a positive impact on human development.

---

[13] Transparency International
[14] It is available since 1984 from International Country Risk Guide.

Some authors have distinguished the terms resource endowments and resource dependent. Because countries depend heavily on its primary sector thus that country is considered as resource rich. But it is also possible that resource abundant country has small primary sector. Ning Ding et al (2005) used three models to investigate the role of natural resource in economic growth and used the data of natural resource assets published by the World Bank. Resource dependent is defined as a proportion of total capital that is accounted for by the natural resource capital. Resource endowment is natural resource capital per capita for the year of 1994[15]. The results of the first Model consistent with Sachs and Warner (1995), Resource endowment variable's coefficient is positive and significant. Results showed a negative coefficient of resource dependence and positive coefficient of resource abundance and both results are significant. In the third model author included a stock of human capital. Neither the resource dependence nor resource endowments have significant impact on growth. Resource endowment has a significant and positive impact on resource dependence but not effect on human capital variable.

Some authors have classified the natural resource according to its geographical base and argued that if natural resources are clustered then it is easier to grab and control. The more pointy resources[16] are controlled by certain groups and production decreases which lead to inequality between tribes (Wick et al 2006). The countries with abundant point resources may lead to low level of institutions and bad governance. Point resources promote the autocrats attribute of a regime and diffuse resource[17] are associated with democracy [Wick et al (2006)].

Murshed (2004) took the data of 91 countries for the sample 1970-2000 and divided the export commodities into various sources; point source natural resources, diffuse-source natural resources, coffee/coca and manufacturing. By using the random effect model, he found those point source commodities are less harmful to democracy than diffuse sources however resource rich countries performed poorly with both diffuse and point sources. So the type of resource endowments partially explains the evolution of democracy and institutions.

Some empirical studies have estimated the resource using sample of single country. Papyrakis et al (2004) have empirical investigated resource curse in the United States, used

---

[15] World Bank dataset, 1994
[16] Point resources are those extracted from narrow geographical or economic base, such as oil or minerals.
[17] Example of diffuse resources is livestock or agriculture produce.

21

the methodology of Mo (2000; 2001) and incorporates transmission channels which showed growth is affected by income inequality and corruption. Author defined Natural resource abundance as share of primary sector production i.e. Agriculture, fishing, factory and mining. Study found a negative relationship between natural resource abundance and economic growth for the sample period of 1986-2001 for 49 different states. Indirect channels were found in the study i.e. investment, openness, schooling, corruption and innovation. Results indicated that resource abundance reduces investment, openness, schooling, R&D expenditure and increases corruption.

Hussain et al. (2009) used proxy of Sachs & Warner (Export of agriculture, minerals and fuel as a percentage of GDP) to check the impact of resource abundance on economic growth in Pakistan. This study used the following variables in the regression analysis; expenditure on education and health, Inflation, investment, trade openness and Labor force and Growth rate of population. Their OLS estimates found a negative relationship between the share of primary goods as a percentage of GDP and economic growth. Moreover this relationship did not change after including the investment on human capital however resource variable became insignificant in this regression analysis.

Siddiqui et al (2010) examined the relationship between natural resource and growth in Pakistan by using the time series data for 1971-2007. They took resource abundance as share of natural resource exports[18] to gross domestic product and share of natural resource exports to total exports in two different models. Openness and human development variables were used in the regression model. Augmented Dicky Fuller, Phillips-Perron test and Dicky Fuller Generalized Least Square methodology had been used to check the stationarity and its results indicated that variables were stationary at first difference. Results of Johansen maximum likelihood cointegration Approach and Pesaran showed positive relationship between natural resource and growth. Moreover, it was found that Dutch disease does not hold in Pakistan.

Magnus et al. (2010) examined the resource effects in china using the both cross-section and time- series data form 28 provinces. Their results show that resource abundance has positive effect on economic growth while resource dependence negatively affected economic growth. The Resource effect on growth also varies with institutions quality. For provinces with institutional quality below the median, the resource-dependence effect on economic growth

---

[18] agricultural, fuel & minerals and ores & metal

changes from positive to negative, as institutional quality increases. After the 2000 shock resource rent has positive impact on growth but this effect decreased and became negative.

3.5 Conclusion

Empirical literature gave mixed about result of resource curse hypothesis. Some studies have found the negative relationship between natural resource abundance and economic growth while on the other hand some of the studies have indicated positive relationship. It has also been cleared that after using different proxies for resource abundance there are again mix results about resource curse hypothesis. Moreover different methodology have been employed for testing the resource curse hypothesis in which cross-sectional methodology along with Sachs and Warner proxy is at the top that often lead to have a negative relationship between natural resource abundance and economic growth. While results of those studies are different that have either used methodology other than cross-section or have used different proxies i.e. education, institutions and openness.

CHAPTER 4

Data Methodology

4.1 Introduction

While studying the resource curse hypothesis it very important to choose appropriate methodology as results differs with different type of econometric methodology. Most of studies have ignored the theoretical based of resource curse hypothesis. So this chapter is divided into three sections. First section of this chapter portrays the theoretical background of this studies, second section depicts the empirical methodology on the basis of the theoretical model and, finally definitions and source of variables are discussed the third section.

4.2 Theoretical Model

Cavalcantie et al (2011) have developed a theoretical model of in order to test the resource curse hypothesis and argued that empirical literature lacks theoretical background of natural resource and economic growth. To produce the consumption goods, they formed the following production function

$$Y(t) = K(t)^{\alpha 1} O(t)^{\alpha 2} \left(A(t) L(t) \right)^{1 - \alpha 1 - \alpha 2} \tag{1}$$

Where $\alpha 1$, $\alpha 2 > 0$, $\alpha 1 + \alpha 2 < 1$, K(t) is physical capital, L(t) is labor and O(t) is natural resource. The above function exhibits constant return to scale.

Let $\quad r(t) = \alpha 1 \frac{Y(t)^{\alpha 1}}{K(t)}$, $p(t) = \alpha 2 \frac{Y(t)^{\alpha 1}}{O(t)}$, $w(t) = (1 - \alpha 1 - \alpha 2) \frac{Y(t)^{\alpha 1}}{L(t)}$

Where $r(t)$ is rental price of capital, $p(t)$ is rental price of natural resource and $w(t)$ is rental price of labor.

Households are identical infinitely lived with measure one and grows at rate of n and endowed with unit of productive time, $N(t) = N(0) e^{nt}$ where $N(0) = initial\ endowment\ of\ labor$ and initial level of capital stock, K(0).

$$\dot{K}(t) = I^k(t) - \delta K(t) \tag{3}$$

Where $I^k(t) = investment\ in\ physical\ capital.$

$$\int_0^\infty e^{-\rho t} N(t) u(c(t)) dt \tag{4}$$

c(t) is real per capital household consumption, $\rho \ \Box \ 0$ is subjective discount rate. The instantaneous utility function is

24

$$u(c) = \frac{c^{1-\theta}-1}{1-\theta}, \theta > 0 \tag{5}$$

θ is the *coefficent of relative risk aversion*. Households are endowed with both capital and natural resource. Natural resource is extracted at the rate $\gamma(t)$. High investment$I^s(t)$ is required to find new reserves or to develop the old fields and cost of this investment would be $\varphi(\frac{I^s(t)}{S(t)})$ unit of output. It assumed that cost is convex. $\varphi'(.) \geq 0$ *and* $\varphi''(.) \geq 0$, $\varphi(0) = \varphi'(0) = 0$. Stock of natural resource is equal to

$$S(t) = -\gamma(t)S(t) + I^s(t), \tag{6}$$

Initial stock of capital is given S(0). Household chooses the consumption path, natural resource extraction rate, investment in natural resource, capital and stock of natural resource so as to maximize

Max

$$\int_0^\infty e^{-\rho t} Nu(c)dt \text{ s.t} \tag{7}$$

$$Nc + Nc + \dot{K} + I^s \left(1 + \emptyset\left(\frac{I^s}{S}\right)\right) = wN + rK - \delta K + p\delta S, \tag{8}$$

$$S = -\dot{\gamma}S + I^s, \tag{9}$$

$$cc \geq 0, \gamma \geq 0, I^s > 0$$

After solving the maximization equation 7 subject to equation 8 and 9, steady state equation of the problem implies that natural resource extraction does not vary along the balanced growth path. Output and natural resource per capita grow at the rate of technological progress. (Cavalcantie et al 2011),

Non- zero balanced growth path equilibrium is saddle path stable if prices of natural resource is determined in the international market.

So long run relationship is found between natural resource and economic growth. By putting the steady state equation author found the following equation that could be estimated for the panel model.

$$\ln y_t = \frac{(1-\alpha_1-\alpha_2)}{(1-\alpha_1)} \ln A_0 - \frac{\alpha_1}{(1-\alpha_1)} \ln(g+n+\delta) + \frac{(1-\alpha_1-\alpha_2)}{(1-\alpha_1)} gt + \frac{\alpha_1}{(1-\alpha_1)} \ln\left(\frac{I_t^k}{Y_t}\right) +$$

$$\frac{\alpha_2}{(1-\alpha_1)} \ln \frac{N_t}{Y_t}$$

$$(10)$$

Where the small letters are in per capita forms, N is natural resource and I_t^k is investment. This equation states the long run relationship between GDP per capita, Investment share of GDP and real value of Natural resource production per capita.

25

4.3 Empirical Methodology

Theoretical model mentioned in previous section and equation 10 suggested that there is long run relationship between natural resource and economic growth, so

$$Y = f(N, X) \qquad (11)$$

Y is the GDP per capita which is function of Natural resource and control variables X and empirical model for panel data becomes as follow.

$$(12)$$

This equation states that GDP per capita depends upon the natural resource and other control variable. In order to find the relationship between natural resource and GDP per capita growth, following equation is formed for regression analysis

$$(13)$$

Now this equation states that GDP per capita growth depends upon the initial income, natural resource, , and other explainatory variables denoted by . Other exogenous variables are; Human capital, Investment, Openness, institutions and terms of trade. After including the control variables in regression model, equation for estimation becomes as follows

$$(14)$$

Where i is country index and it indicates the number of the cross sectional regression of the panel. So dependent variable is , , GDP per capita growth and independent or explaintory variables are:

 = Initial income

N_{it} = Natural resource variables

H_{it} = Human capital measured as School enrollment primary (% gross)

I_{it} = Investment measured as fixed capital formation capital

opn_{it} = Openness measured as Export plus import divided by GDP

Ins_{it} = Institutional Quality measured by corruption index

26

TOT_{it} = Terms of Trade

G is economic growth which is function of natural resource abundance and other control variables. The first control variable is lag GDP per capita which is called initial income in literature of conditional convergence theory. This variable will confirm the conditional convergence of countries as in 1960s growth theories were mainly of neoclassical model and developed by Solow(1956), Ramsey (1928) Swan(1956), and these models have considered conditional convergence property which states that the countries with low level of initial real GDP per capital will grow faster. If all countries are same, having same economic features, then poor will grow faster than rich one, it is called Absolute Convergence. When countries are different in various aspects, then convergence will be conditional. As we are taking in account other control/explainatroy variables which are different in each country, so regression model will verify conditional convergence hypothesis (Barro 1996).

N_{it} is set of natural resource variables in a country and measured with total natural resource rent as percentage of GDP which include both renewable (oil, gas, minerals, coal) and non-renewable natural resource (forest). This variable will tell us the impact of both renewable and non-renewable resource on growth. Total natural resource will also be decomposed into oil rent, gas rent, and mineral rent. Ambiguous relationship between natural resource abundance and economic growth is found as Sachs et al (1995, 2001) and Gylfason (2000, 2007) found negative relationship between two variables whereas studies Martin et al (2003), Stijns (2006) and Brunnschweiler (2008) found positive relationship between variables

Most of theoretical literature of growth model have emphasized on capital accumulation. It has been argued that building up stocks of capital will increase the productivity and will enhance the capacity to build further stocks. Continuous investment will generate continuous growth in the long run. Three forms of capital is discussed by the Barro (1996). First one is physical capital which is developed by making the investment in equipment and structures. Second form is human capital which is produced by education, training and learning by doing. Third form is disembodied knowledge, which is made by research and development. So this study have included two types of capital accumulation; investment and human capital. There is strong positive relationship between human capital and economic growth (Barro , 1996). Human capital is measured by primary school enrolment as a % of gross Investment

27

measured by Gross fixed capital formation. Human capital and investment could be channel of resource curse. When manufacturing or traded sector develop then there will be increase in the human capital accumulation. In contrast, when non-traded sector expands as a result of resource boom then employment in the traded sector will decline; thus hence low economic growth (Sachs and Warner, 1999).

Theoretical literature on trade growth model can be classified into two sorts. The advocates of Adam Smith argue that trade will increase productivity through learning by doing or through specialization in research. They rely on spillover mechanism that generates cumulative increase in productivity and specialization. Second theory of trade growth model is Comparative advantage which leads to specialization in particular sector. Some countries will grow faster than other countries as some sectors generate high rate of productivity. So trade is important determinant of economic growth and this study included openness variable as a measure of trade liberalization. Openness and economic growth is positively related to each other as found in much empirical literature (Barro 1996). Terms of trade can also influence the economic growth both positively and negatively.

Next variable in empirical model is quality of institutions which we measured by corruption index. Literature has emphasized the institution as main determinant of economic growth and also considered as a major cause of resource curse. [Torvik (2002), Martin et al (2003)]. Institutions and governance are important channel of resource curse and polices could undermine the social welfare goal in resource rich countries where institutions are not very strong (Martin et al 2003). Point resources such as oil, mineral and gas can create monopoly, control by small group of people, provoke rent seeking activates and thus have negative impact on welfare of overall society (Torvik 2002).

4.32 Interaction Model

To see how corruption will impact the relationship between natural resource rent and economic, an interaction term is introduced within the model i.e.

$$G_{it} = c_i + \alpha_1 \ln y_{it-1} + \alpha_2 N_{it} + \alpha_3 H_{it} + \alpha_4 I_{it} + \alpha_5 opn_{it} + \alpha_6 Ins_{it} + \alpha_7 TOT_{it} + \alpha_8 N_{it} Ins_{it} + u_{it} \qquad (15)$$

4.31 Regional Analysis

In order to see the relationship between natural resource rent and economic growth in different regions of the world, we have incorporated set of slope regional dummies in our model one by one. Seven regression equations will be estimated of slope regional dummies which are as follows:

$$G_{it} = c_i + \alpha_1 \ln y_{it-1} + \alpha_2 N_{it} + \alpha_3 H_{it} + \alpha_4 I_{it} + \alpha_5 opn_{it} + \alpha_6 Ins_{it} + \alpha_7 TOT_{it} + \alpha_8 N_{it} D_1 + u_{it} \tag{16}$$

$$D_1 = 1 \; if \; it \; is \; South \; Asia \; other \; wise \; D_1 = 0$$

$$G_{it} = c_i + \alpha_1 \ln y_{it-1} + \alpha_2 N_{it} + \alpha_3 H_{it} + \alpha_4 I_{it} + \alpha_5 opn_{it} + \alpha_6 Ins_{it} + \alpha_7 TOT_{it} + \alpha_8 N_{it} D_2 + u_{it} \tag{17}$$

$$D_2 = 1 \; if \; it \; is \; North \; America \; other \; wise \; D_2 = 0$$

$$G_{it} = c_i + \alpha_1 \ln y_{it-1} + \alpha_2 N_{it} + \alpha_3 H_{it} + \alpha_4 I_{it} + \alpha_5 opn_{it} + \alpha_6 Ins_{it} + \alpha_7 TOT_{it} + \alpha_8 N_{it} D_3 + u_{it} \tag{18}$$

$$D_3 = 1 \; if \; it \; is \; Middle \; East \; and \; North \; Africa \; otherwise \; D_3 = 0$$

$$G_{it} = c_i + \alpha_1 \ln y_{it-1} + \alpha_2 N_{it} + \alpha_3 H_{it} + \alpha_4 I_{it} + \alpha_5 opn_{it} + \alpha_6 Ins_{it} + \alpha_7 TOT_{it} + \alpha_8 N_{it} D_4 + u_{it} \tag{19}$$

$$D_4 = 1 \; if \; it \; is \; Europe \; and \; Central \; Asia \; otherwise \; D_4 = 0$$

$$G_{it} = c_i + \alpha_1 \ln y_{it-1} + \alpha_2 N_{it} + \alpha_3 H_{it} + \alpha_4 I_{it} + \alpha_5 opn_{it} + \alpha_6 Ins_{it} + \alpha_7 TOT_{it} + \alpha_8 N_{it} D_5 + u_{it} \tag{20}$$

$$D_5 = 1 \; if \; it \; is \; Sub \; Saharan \; Africa \; otherwise \; D_5 = 0$$

$$G_{it} = c_i + \alpha_1 \ln y_{it-1} + \alpha_2 N_{it} + \alpha_3 H_{it} + \alpha_4 I_{it} + \alpha_5 opn_{it} + \alpha_6 Ins_{it} + \alpha_7 TOT_{it} + \alpha_8 N_{it} D_6 + u_{it} \tag{21}$$

$$D_6 = 1 \; if \; it \; is \; Latin \; America \; and \; Caribbean \; otherwise \; D_6 = 0$$

$$G_{it} = c_i + \alpha_1 \ln y_{it-1} + \alpha_2 N_{it} + \alpha_3 H_{it} + \alpha_4 I_{it} + \alpha_5 opn_{it} + \alpha_6 Ins_{it} +$$
$$\alpha_7 TOT_{it} + \alpha_8 N_{it} D_7 + u_{it} \qquad (22)$$

$$D_7 = 1 \; if \; it \; is \; \text{East Asia and Pacific} \; otherwise \; D_7 = 0$$

Similarly, slope dummies of different income group level and a dummy of Muslim countries will also be introduced.

4.4 Econometric Methodology

This section describes different methods to estimate the panel data and

4.41 Panel Data

This study employs the panel data model which contains time series observation of number of countries and captures both individual-specific effects and time effects. It is called longitudinal data/ cross-sectional time series. If time series are same for all cross-section then data is called balanced panel data and if some observations are missing then it is called unbalanced panel data.

There are some advantages of panel data. It takes into account of heterogeneity explicitly as number of observations is much higher in panel data set than in cross-section or time series data set and it gives more variability, high degree of freedom, more efficiency and alleviates multicollinearity. (Kennedy et al 2008).

Wooldridge et.al (2002) used the following functional form for the unobserved effect model.

$$y_{it} = x_{it}\beta + c_i + u_{it} \qquad (23)$$

Our model

$$G_{it} = c_i + \alpha_1 Y_{it-1} + \alpha_2 N_{it} + \alpha_3 H_{it} + \alpha_4 I_{it} + \alpha_5 opn_{it} + \alpha_6 Ins_{it} + \alpha_7 TOT_{it} +$$
$$u_{it}$$

$$\qquad (24)$$

t= 1991, 1992............2011 ;   i= 1, 2 170

30

Where $\alpha_1, \alpha_2, \alpha_3, \alpha_4, \alpha_5, \alpha_6, \alpha_7$ are the parameters. $Y_{it-1}, N_{it}, H_{it}, I_{it}, opn_{it}, Ins_{it}, TOT_{it}$ are the explanatory variables and they can change their values both at across countries i and across time t. The c_i is unobserved effect which is called individual effect or individual heterogeneity when i is indexed as individuals. The u_{it} change both across t and i and it is called idiosyncratic error/ or idiosyncratic disturbances. These idiosyncratic disturbances are independent and identically distributed. Now the question is how to treat with c_i? If we treat c_i as fixed (it varies across group or time periods) then the model will be called Fixed Effect Model and if c_i is treated as random then the above model will be called Random Effect Model. If model contains no individual effect then Ordinary Least Squares (OLS) parameters are efficient and consistent and OLS's five assumptions are; Linearity, exogeneity, homoscedasticity, no autocorrelation, observations on the independent variable are fixed in repeated sampling and full rank. (Greene, 2003; Kennedy, 2008).

4.42 Fixed Effect Model

There are many ways for estimating fixed effect model. Least Square Dummy Variable model (LSDV), Within Effect Model and Between Effect Model.

Functional form of Least Square Dummy Variable is as follow:

$$G_{it} = c_2 D_{2i} + c_3 D_{3i} + \ldots\ldots + c_n D_{ni} + \alpha_1 Y_{it-1} + \alpha_2 N_{it} + \alpha_3 H_{it} + \alpha_4 I_{it} + \alpha_5 opn_{it} +$$
$$\alpha_6 Ins_{it} + \alpha_6 TOT_{it} + u_{it}$$
$$(25)$$

Where D_{1i} is dummy variable that takes the value 1 if i = 1 and 0 other wise. D_{2i} =1 for country 2 i.e. i=2 and so on. These dummies will capture all the individual effect. In order to avoid the problem of dummy variable trap we have removed the intercept. This approach is relatively easy but it creates problems when there are many groups in the panel. Only coefficient of regressors are consistent when T is fixed and nT $\to\infty$. Coefficients of dummy variables are not consistent because number of parameters increases when nT increases and this problem is called incidental parameter problem. (Baltagi 2001)

31

4.43 Within Group Effect Model

Within group effect model does not require dummy variables. It is within transformation as it subtracts each value of cross-sectional object from time-mean of the variable. This transformation will remove incidental parameter problem and run OLS on the following model to compute the parameters.

$$G_{it} - \bar{G}_{i\,\blacksquare} = \alpha_1(Y_{it-1} - \bar{Y}_{i\,\blacksquare}) + \alpha_2(N_{it} - \bar{N}_{i\,\blacksquare}) + \alpha_3(H_{it} - \bar{H}_{i\,\blacksquare}) + \alpha_4(I_{it} - \bar{I}_{i\,\blacksquare}) + \alpha_5(Opn_{it} - \overline{Opn}_{i\,\blacksquare}) + \alpha_6(Ins_{it} - \overline{Ins}_{i\,\blacksquare}) + \alpha_7(TOT_{it} - \overline{TOT}_{i\,\blacksquare}) + (u_{it} - \bar{u}_{i\,\blacksquare})$$

(26)

$\bar{G}_{i\,\blacksquare}$ is dependent variable mean of group i. $\bar{Y}_{i\,\blacksquare}, \bar{N}_{i\,\blacksquare}, \bar{H}_{i\,\blacksquare}, \bar{I}_{i\,\blacksquare}, \overline{Opn}_{i\,\blacksquare}, \overline{Ins}_{i\,\blacksquare}, \overline{TOT}_{i\,\blacksquare}$ are mean of independent variables of group i. The within effect model has some disadvantages. This model does not report dummy coefficient and it has large degree of freedom for error which results into small MSE and smaller standard errors for the parameters estimates.

In between group effect model, we use group means of the dependent and independent variable and it reduces the number of observation up to n. Then run OLS on the following model.

$$\bar{G}_{i\,\blacksquare} = c + (\bar{Y}_{i\,\blacksquare}) + (\bar{N}_{i\,\blacksquare}) + (\bar{H}_{i\,\blacksquare}) + (\bar{I}_{i\,\blacksquare}) + \alpha_5(\overline{Opn}_{i\,\blacksquare}) + (\overline{Ins}_{i\,\blacksquare}) + (TOT_{it} - \overline{TOT}_{i\,\blacksquare}) + (\bar{u}_{i\,\blacksquare})$$

(27)

Fixed effect transformation removes the individual effect. Another method used to remove the individual is first differencing method but the difference lies between two estimates when time period is greater than 2. If there are only two time periods then two estimators are same (Jeffrey M. Wooldridge, 2002).

4.44 Testing Group Effect

Rewriting equation (24)

$$G_{it} = c_2 D_{2i} + c_3 D_{3i} + \ldots\ldots + c_n D_{ni} + \alpha_1 Y_{it-1} + \alpha_2 N_{it} + \alpha_3 H_{it} + \alpha_4 I_{it} + \alpha_5 opn_{it}$$
$$+ \alpha_6 Ins_{it} + \alpha_6 TOT_{it} + u_{it}$$

The null hypothesis is that all the coefficients of dummy variables are equal to zero. Remember that above has no intercept. If we include the intercept than there must be n-1 dummies in order to avoid the dummy trap.

Ho: $c_1 = \cdots = c_n = 0$ F test is used to test this hypothesis.[19]

$$\frac{(e'e_{Efficient} - e'e_{Robust})/(n)}{(e'e_{Robust})/(nT-n-k)} = \frac{(R2_{Robust} - R2_{Efficient})/(n)}{(1-R2_{Robust})/(nT-n-k)} \sim F(n, nT-n-k) \qquad (28)$$

If the null hypothesis is rejected then fixed effect model is better than pooled OLS model i.e. all coefficients of dummy variables are not equal to zero and if the null hypothesis is not rejected then the pooled OLS is better than the fixed effect model.

4.45 Fixed Time Effect

In time fixed effect model intercepts vary over time and assumed constant across the individuals/countries at each given point in time.

$$G_{it} = \lambda_t + \alpha_1 Y_{it-1} + \alpha_2 N_{it} + \alpha_3 H_{it} + \alpha_4 I_{it} + \alpha_5 opn_{it} + \alpha_6 Ins_{it} + \alpha_7 TOT_{it} + u_{it}$$
$$(29)$$

λ_t is time-varying intercept. In the group effect model, individual dummies were included to capture the individual effect. If we include time dummies in the LSDV model instead of individual dummies then the model becomes fixed time effect model of LSDV.

$$G_{it} = \lambda_1 D_{2i} + \lambda_2 D_{3i} + \ldots\ldots + \lambda_t D_{ni} + \alpha_1 Y_{it-1} + \alpha_2 N_{it} + \alpha_3 H_{it} + \alpha_4 I_{it} + \alpha_5 opn_{it} +$$
$$\alpha_6 Ins_{it} + \alpha_6 TOT_{it} + u_{it}$$
$$(30)$$

D_{1t} take the value 1 for the first period and zero otherwise and so on.

Within time effect model:

---

[19] Efficient model in the above F-test is pooled regression and the robust model is LSDV(or within effect model)

$$G_{it} - \bar{G}_{\blacksquare t} = \alpha_1(Y_{it-1} - \bar{Y}_{\blacksquare t}) + \alpha_2(N_{it} - \bar{N}_{\blacksquare t}) + \alpha_3(H_{it} - \bar{H}_{\blacksquare t}) + \alpha_4(I_{it} - \bar{I}_{\blacksquare t}) +$$
$$\alpha_5(Opn_{it} - \overline{Opn}_{\blacksquare t}) + \alpha_6(Ins_{it} - \overline{Ins}_{\blacksquare t}) + \alpha_7(TOT_{it} - \overline{TOT}_{\blacksquare t}) + (u_{it} - \bar{u}_{\blacksquare t})$$

(31)

Between time effect model:

$$\bar{G}_{\blacksquare t} = c + (\bar{Y}_{\blacksquare t}) + (\bar{N}_{\blacksquare t}) + (\bar{H}_{\blacksquare t}) + (\bar{I}_{\blacksquare t}) + \alpha_5(\overline{Opn}_{\blacksquare t}) + (\overline{Ins}_{\blacksquare t}) + (TOT_{it} -$$
$$\overline{TOT}_{\blacksquare t}) + (\bar{u}_{\blacksquare t})$$

(32)

To test whether there exist time effect or not, we will test the coefficients of time dummies used in equation 8

Ho= λ_1=.....=λ_t=0

F-test: $\dfrac{(e'e_{pooled} - e'e_{within})/(n)}{(e'e_{within})/(nT-n-k)}$ ~ F(n, nT-n-k) (33)

If we reject the null hypothesis then the time effect is better than pooled OLS model.

4.46 Two Way Fixed Effect model

When intercepts vary both across countries and time the fixed effect model can be written as:

$$G_{it} = c_i + \lambda_t + \alpha_1 Y_{it-1} + \alpha_2 N_{it} + \alpha_3 H_{it} + \alpha_4 I_{it} + \alpha_5 opn_{it} + \alpha_6 Ins_{it} + \alpha_7 TOT_{it} + u_{it}$$
(34)

For within effect model:

$$G*_{it} = G_{it} - \bar{G}_{i\blacksquare} - \bar{G}_{\blacksquare t} + \bar{G}_{\blacksquare\blacksquare}$$

$$Y*_{it-1} = Y_{it-1} - \bar{Y}_{i\blacksquare} - \bar{Y}_{\blacksquare t-1} + \bar{Y}_{\blacksquare\blacksquare}$$

$$N*_{it} = N_{it} - \bar{N}_{i\blacksquare} - \bar{N}_{\blacksquare t} + \bar{N}_{\blacksquare\blacksquare}$$

$$H*_{it} = H_{it} - \bar{H}_{i\blacksquare} - \bar{H}_{\blacksquare t} + \bar{H}_{\blacksquare\blacksquare}$$

$$I*_{it} = I_{it} - \bar{I}_{i\blacksquare} - \bar{I}_{\blacksquare t} + \bar{I}_{\blacksquare\blacksquare}$$

$$\text{Ins }*_{it} = \text{Ins}_{it} - \overline{Ins}_{i\blacksquare} - \overline{Ins}_{\blacksquare t} + \overline{Ins}_{\blacksquare\blacksquare}$$

$$\text{Opn }*_{it} = \text{Opn}_{it} - \overline{Opn}_{i\blacksquare} - \overline{Opn}_{\blacksquare t} + \overline{Opn}_{\blacksquare\blacksquare}$$

$$\text{TOT }*_{it} = \text{TOT}_{it} - \overline{TOT}_{i\blacksquare} - \overline{TOT}_{\blacksquare t} + \overline{TOT}_{\blacksquare\blacksquare}$$

Where $\bar{G}_{\blacksquare\blacksquare}$ is overall mean of the dependent variable and $\bar{Y}_{\blacksquare\blacksquare}, \bar{N}_{\blacksquare\blacksquare}, \bar{H}_{\blacksquare\blacksquare}, \bar{I}_{\blacksquare\blacksquare}, \overline{Ins}_{\blacksquare\blacksquare}, \overline{Opn}_{\blacksquare\blacksquare}, \overline{TOT}_{\blacksquare\blacksquare}$ are overall mean of independent variables.

The null hypothesis for both fixed time and group effect is as follows:

Ho= $\lambda_1 = \ldots = \lambda_t = 0$ and $c_1 = \cdots = c_n = 0$

F-test: $\dfrac{(e'e_{Efficient} - e'e_{Robust})/(n+T)}{(e'e_{Robust})/(nT-n-T-k+1)} \sim F[(n+T), (nT\text{-}n\text{-}k+1)]$ (35)

4.47 Testing Random Effects (LM test)

Breusch and Pagan (1980) developed the Langrange Multilplier (LM) test to test whether cross-sectional variance components are zero or not? So the null hypothesis is Ho: $\sigma_c^2 = 0$. LM follows χ-squared distribution with one degree of freedom.

$$LM_c = \frac{nT}{2(T-1)}\left[\frac{e'DDe}{e'e} - 1\right]^2 = \frac{nT}{2(T-1)}\left[\frac{T^2\bar{e}'\bar{e}}{e'e} - 1\right]^2 \sim \chi^2(1)$$ (36)

$\bar{e}$ is n×1 vector of the group specific means of pooled regression residuals and $e'e$ is the SSE of the pooled OLS regression. We can also test two way random effect model has the null hypothesis of Ho: $\sigma_{c1}^2 = 0$ and $\sigma_{c2}^2 = 0$.

$$LM_{c12} = LM_{c1} + LM_{c2} \sim \chi^2(2)$$ (37)

4.48 Hausman Test: Fixed Effects versus Random Effects

If the individual effects are correlated with other regressors than the random effect model gives biased estimators. So we will prefer fixed effect model. Hausman test is used under the null hypothesis that individual effect is uncorrelated with other regressors .

$$m = (b_{robust} - b_{efficient}) \Sigma^{-1}(b_{robust} - b_{efficient}) \sim \chi^2(k)$$ (38)

$\Sigma^{-1}(b_{robust} - b_{efficient}) = \mathrm{Var}(b_{robust}) - \mathrm{Var}(b_{efficient})$ is the difference in the estimate covariance matrix of the parameter estimates between LSDV model[20] and random effect model[21]

4.5 Data and Variables

This section will discuss the variables used in regression analysis. Each variable is explained by definition. Main focused variables are growth and natural resources but some other variables are also used which are main determinant of economic growth.

Annual percentage growth rate of GDP per capita has taken to measure the economic growth of a country and it is calculated by simple growth formula which is equal to is: [current GDP per capita – previous year GDP per capita]/ [previous year GDP per capita]. GDP per capita is estimated by dividing the GDP to population. Data of annual percentage growth rate of GDP per capita has been taken from World Development Index from 1991 to 2011 for all 170 countries.

To check the conditional hypothesis, study included initial income in the regression model and this variable is calculated by taking lag of GDP per capita from 1991 to 2011 and this variable is in log form. Data of GDP per capita is available in World Development Index.

The most important variables of this study are different types of natural resource rents which are main concern of this study and these resource rents are calculated by subtracting the value of production at world price from total cost of production. This study has employed four types of natural resource rents in the regression model. We get the total natural resources rents, by adding both renewable[22] and nonrenewable natural resource[23]. Mineral[24] rents are calculated by subtracting the value of production for minerals from total costs of production. Methods to calculate the natural resource rent is explained in the "The Changing Wealth of Nations: Measuring Sustainable Development in the New Millennium", World Bank.

---

[20] Robust
[21] Efficient
[22] forest rents
[23] coal rents, mineral rents, oil rents, natural gas rents,
[24] silver, bauxite, lead, zinc, iron, gold, Tin, copper, nickel, and phosphate

Gross enrollment ratio is taken as a proxy to measure the education level in a country which is the ratio of total enrollment to the population and no specific age group has been taken.

Gross capital formation variable has been used as a measure of investment level in a country and formerly this variable was called as gross domestic investment. It includes net change in the inventories and fixed assets which consist of land improvements, machinery, equipment purchases, plant, private residential, railways, construction of offices, schools, hospitals and commercial buildings. To meet the unforeseen changes in the future, firms hold the stock of goods; these goods are included in the inventories. Net procurements of antiques are also included in capital formation. Gross capital formation has been taken form WDI.

Openness variable is ratio of export plus import to GDP and barter term of trade index is measured by taking ratio of unit value indexes to import unit value index with 2000 year as a base. The data of exports and imports of goods and services are taken from WDI.

To measure the institutions quality, corruption is used the regression model which is taken from International Country Risk Guide (ICRG) for the period 1990 to 2008.

CHAPTER 5

Results and Discussion

5.1 Introduction

After choosing appropriate econometric methodology, now this chapter will discuss empirical findings of current study including group effect test, to see either the pool is preferred over panel or not? Results of Hasumen test is also shown to make a decision between fixed and random effect model

5.2 Group Effect Test

Current study has used Dummy Least Square model to check group effect and Wald test is applied to check either the joint coefficients of all intercept are equal to zero or not. Result of this test is shown below.

Table: 5.1

F-test for no fixed effect				F-test for no time effect			
Num DF	Den DF	F- value	Prob > F	Num DF	Den DF	F- value	Prob > F
121	1287	5.01	0.0000	17	1391	7.16	0.0000

Table 5.1 shows the values of F-stats and p-value suggest rejecting the null hypothesis of no group effect and it lead to admit that Pooled regression is not better than fixed effect model. Secondly, study test the time effect that will be helpful to decide either the intercept vary across the time or not. Results in table showed that we can reject the null hypothesis of no time effect as value of p-value is almost equal to zero. These results suggest that simple pooled regression is not better than fixed time effect. Finally, it can be concluded that pooling is not appropriate in this particular case because intercept can vary both across the countries or across the time and it will be plausible and quite suitable to apply either fixed or random effect model. For this purpose Hausaman Test is used to decide whether fixed effect or random effect model is appropriate for this given model.

5.3 Hausaman Test

Hausaman Test states that, if the individual effects are correlated with regressors then fixed effect is better than the random effect model and in this case random effect model give bias result that can be seen in table 5.3 where p value of Chi-square is equal to zero which rejects the null hypothesis of Hausaman test.

Table: 5.2

	Coefficients			
	(α*)	(β**)	(α -β)	sqrt(diag(V_α -V_ β))
	fixed group		Difference	S.E.
Initial Income	-4.11827	-0.3109	-3.8072	0.75489
Investment	0.13487	0.1364	-0.0015	0.0111
Education	0.04707	0.0341	0.0128	0.0058
Corruption	-0.7518	-0.4385	-0.3132	0.0862
Terms of trade	-0.0008	0.0088	-0.0096	0.0026
Openness	0.00080	0.0007	0.00008	0.0002
Total natural resource rent	0.1719	0.0349	0.1369	0.0258
chi2(7)	64.25			
Prob	0.0000			

* α = consistent under Ho and Ha

** β = inconsistent under Ha, efficient under Ho

Ho: difference in coefficients not systematic

5.4 Estimation results and Discussion

There are different methods to estimate the panel data but the Hausman test suggested that fixed effect is appropriate for estimation of the model of current study. The regression model is estimated by using within effect model, time effect model, between effect and two way within effect model but estimation results of only within effect model are shown because these are more accurate and significant as compare to the rest of methodologies.

Control variables of the estimated model are; initial income, education, investment, corruption, openness and terms of trade. Empirical results showed that initial income is negatively related to GDP per capita growth which confirms the conditional convergence hypothesis i.e. countries with low level of initial income will grow faster as compare to the countries with high initial income [Barrow (1996)]. Coefficient of initial income indicates that if initial income increase by one percent then GDP growth will decrease by 4.11 percent. This result remains negative and significant in all the regressions. Investment, education and openness are highly significant and positive correlated to the GDP per capita growth. Relationship remains positive and significant in all other regression, only a slight change in coefficient is observed. Investment in country increases the level of output in an economy because it generates employment opportunities which enhance the GDP per capita growth (Barro, 1996). Terms of trade is significant in 3rd and 4th regression of table 5.5 and is positive correlated to economic growth. Corruption found to be negatively correlated to economic growth as it reduces the incentive and opportunity of investment and innovation (North, 1990) and it remains sticky in its direction and level of significance. Results suggest that on average, GDP per capita growth decreases by 0.75 percent when corruption increases by one unit. Finally, it is depicted by the empirical procedure that model of current study is 45% explained by its explanatory variables as R-square in all regression remains the constant in its magnitude i.e. 0.45.

Estimations result in table 5.4 suggest that total natural resource rents are positively correlated to GDP per capita growth which is highly significant and positive related to GDP per capita growth. Results indicate that renewable[25] and non-renewable resources[26] have positive impact on the economic growth. Coefficient of total natural resource rent shows that if total natural resource rent increases by one unit then the GDP per capita growth will increase by 0.17 percent. This positive relationship does not change when we incorporate other control variables whereas the value of coefficient changes with every control variable. Inclusion of Initial income, human capital and investment in the model cause coefficient of total natural resource rent to rise whereas corruption causes the coefficient to decrease which suggest that corruption could be possible channels [see appendix table 5.3].

Graphical analysis also showed the same results and indicates positive and linear relationship between economic growth and all the types of natural resource rent (see appendix graph 1, 2, 3). Total natural resource is also decomposed into Oil, gas and mineral rents and Oil rent. Estimation results in table 5.5 shows that Oil rents have stronger impact on the economic growth (with a significant coefficient of 0.27). Moreover Gas rents are positively but insignificantly correlated and Mineral rents are also positively and significantly correlated with GDP per capita growth.

---

[25] Forest
[26] Oil, mineral, gas and coal

40

Thus it has been cleared that empirical findings of current study are unable to support the resource curse hypothesis and lie in the line of an immense literature of resource blessing. Davis (1995), Martin et al (2003) Stijn (2006), Brunnschweiler et al (2008) and Manzano et al (2011) also find the same results in one or another way. There can be two possible reasons of rejecting the resource hypothesis. First reason can be the difference of methodology because mostly cross-sectional studies favor the resource curse hypothesis [Sachs et al, (1995), (2001); Gylfason, (2000), (2001), (2007); Da Cunha Leite (2001); Atkinson et al (2003); Martin et al (2003); Papyrakis et al (2004)]. In Cross-sectional models, numbers of observation are usually less than panel data as omitted variable bias can affect the outcome.

There are a few studies which use Panel technique; however it makes the outcome more reliable because lager data set has more variability and less collinearity (Mills et al 2006). That is why current study concentrated more on this technique secondly current study has used a different proxy for resource variables. Most of the literature have used ratio of primary product exports to GDP as a measure of resource abundance and it does not represent the resource abundance rather than resource dependence (Brunnschweiler et al 2008).

Our results are based on large sample, a comprehensive natural resource variable and a different technique that may be able me to empirically conclude that natural resources itself are not curse. Although all countries in the sample are not rich in natural resource but it is observed from data that resource abundant countries have high natural resource rents because of having economies of scale in natural resource extraction.

Table 5.4 Total Natural resource rents, oil rents, mineral rents, gas rents and economic growth

	(1) GDP per capita growth	(2) GDP per capita growth	(3) GDP per capita growth	(4) GDP per capita growth
Initial income	-4.1183***	-3.8482***	-3.9736***	-4.2629***
	(0.7705)	(0.7458)	(0.7614)	(0.7852)
Education	0.0471***	0.0358**	0.0342*	0.0465***
	(0.0107)	(0.0130)	(0.0134)	(0.0109)
Investment	0.1349***	0.1768***	0.1634***	0.1160***
	(0.0254)	(0.0278)	(0.0286)	(0.0256)
Corruption	-0.7519***	-0.6423***	-0.6455***	-0.8362***
	(0.1579)	(0.1568)	(0.1611)	(0.1591)
Openness	0.0008*	0.0015***	0.0019***	0.0009**
	(0.0003)	(0.0004)	(0.0004)	(0.0003)
Terms of Trade	-0.0008	-0.0016	0.0133**	0.0115*
	(0.0056)	(0.0053)	(0.0047)	(0.0050)
Total Natural Resource rent	0.1719***			
	(0.0303)			
Oil rent		0.2620***		
		(0.0406)		
Gas rent			0.1128	
			(0.0643)	
Mineral rent				0.1968**
				(0.0604)
_cons	26.5702***	24.5206***	25.1490***	28.1335***
	(5.7921)	(5.7698)	(5.8977)	(5.9616)
N	1416	1243	1237	1416
R^2	0.426	0.474	0.457	0.416

Standard errors in parentheses, $p < 0.05$, $p < 0.01$, $p < 0.001$

Since empirical procedure mentioned in above table represents that natural resource rents do not harm the economic growth directly however it can affect the economic growth via institutions. Interaction term of corruption is introduced which showed that countries where corruption is high, natural resource rent will negatively impact the economic growth [see appendix table 5.8] and this empirical finding are very similar to the Da Cunha Leite et al (1999) and Sala-i-Martin et al (2003) who are of the view that corruption found to be the main channel of resource curse.

Regional analysis of resource curse hypothesis in current study also depict that negative relationship is found only in the South Asia regions and this region has high corruption along with the low level of governance. Average level of governance index in South Asia is below 8 while in other regions this figure is above 8 (ICRG, 2008). Total seven of the regional dummies for South Asia, North America, Middle East and North Africa, Europe and Central Asia, Sub Saharan Africa, Latin America & Caribbean and East Asia Pacific was introduced that can be viewed in appendix table 5.5. These results of the said table also indicate that magnitude of relationship differs across North America, Middle East and North Africa, Europe and Central Asia, Sub Saharan Africa, Latin America & Caribbean and East Asia Pacific.

It also noteworthy that positive relationship found in the resource rich regions like Middle East and North Africa; Sub Saharan Africa. These regions are rich in their natural resource and our results depicts that there is positive relationship between total natural resource rent and economic growth and also between oil rent and economic growth [see appendix table 5.5 and table 5.6] This result shows that resource abundance itself is not bad for any country rather it's the management of natural resources and quality of institutions which makes the country to grow. These results are based on the interaction of total natural resource rents with regional dummies. Results of interaction term of oil rents with regional dummies are shown in the appendix table 5.6 which indicates the same results and again the resource cruse is found in the South Asian countries. A sample of top 40 oil reserve countries is also used in the regression analysis and results are shown in appendix table 5.7. Corruption and education variable become insignificant but relationship between natural resource rents and economic growth remained positive. Investment and openness variable is highly significant and have positive sign in appendix table 5.7. To capture the religion effect, interaction dummy of Muslims countries is introduced but this slope dummy does not come as significant. Resource curse is also analyzed at different income group level and only Middle Income group interaction come out significant which shows that coefficient differ only Middle Income group countries.

CHAPTER 6

Conclusion

Natural resources provide major source of income and employment to the developing countries. It is argued by many studies that countries with abundant of natural resource will grow slower than countries with low level of natural resource and Sachs and Warner (1995)'s study provided a strong empirical base to the resource curse hypothesis which got attention of many reseachers. Number of studies empirically tested resource curse hypothesis and some of them supported the resource curse hypothesis while others did not. Their results remained dependent on the use of proxies and methodologies. So it is very important to choose appropriate methodology and proxy.

The core objective of the study was to investigate the resource curse hypothesis in comprehensive way by using large dataset along with appropriate methodology and suitable proxy for resource variable. This study used different types of natural resource rents as proxies for natural resource variables in a sample of 170 countries from year 1991 to 2011 and employed within effect model for estimation. Results showed that all types of natural resource rents, total natural resource rents, oil rents and mineral rents are positive related to the economic growth thus rejecting the resource curse hypothesis. This argument is also supported by our graphical analysis.

Empirical results revealed that conditional hypothesis holds in given sample of countries. Investment, education and openness have positive contribution in economic growth of a country while corruption has negative impact on the economic performance of the countries. Corruption found as a main channel of resource curse. Our interaction variable showed that natural resources will negatively impact the economic growth in those countries where level of corruption is high.

Moreover, regional analysis of this study indicated that South Asian economies are suffering from resource curse disease and the main reason of this curse is weak institutions. Natural resources contribute positively in those regions where level of institution is relatively better. This analysis clearly shows that it's not only the natural resource which matter for any country but other factors are equally important. So resource curse has strong relationship with level of institution and quality of governance.

44

To check the robustness of our results, sample was reduced to top 40 oil reserve countries which showed that same results about resource curse hypothesis. Only education and corruption variable became insignificant.

Our results are more reliable as most of the resource curse studies have used the cross-sectional data which often lead to bias results and most of the literature used exports of primary products as a proxy of natural resource abundance which is also criticized by some authors by arguing that this proxy does not measure the resource abundance rather resource dependence [Brunnschweiler et al (2008)]

So natural resources itself are not bad for any countries rather it's the management and state of institutions which makes the difference in economic growth of country.

References

Acemoglu, Daron, & Robinson, James A. (2006). Persistence of power, elites and institutions: National Bureau of Economic Research.

Alexeev, Michael, & Conrad, Robert. (2009). The elusive curse of oil. *The Review of Economics and Statistics, 91*(3), 586-598.

Arezki, Rabah, & Van der Ploeg, Frederick. (2007). Can the natural resource curse be turned into a blessing? The role of trade policies and institutions. *The Role of Trade Policies and Institutions (March 2007)., Vol.*

Arezki, Rabah, & van der Ploeg, Frederick. (2010). Trade policies, institutions and the natural resource curse. *Applied Economics Letters, 17*(15), 1443-1451.

Atkinson, Giles, & Hamilton, Kirk. (2003). Savings, growth and the resource curse hypothesis. *World Development, 31*(11), 1793-1807.

Auty, Richard. (2002). *Sustaining development in mineral economies: the resource curse thesis*: Psychology Press.

Auty, Richard M. (1991). Mismanaged mineral dependence: Zambia 1970–90. *Resources Policy, 17*(3), 170-183.

Auty, Richard M. (1994). Industrial policy reform in six large newly industrializing countries: The resource curse thesis. *World development, 22*(1), 11-26.

Auty, Richard M. (1995a). Economic development and the resource curse thesis. *Economic and political reform in developing countries, Houndmills: Macmillan, 58*, 80.

Auty, Richard M. (1995b). Industrial policy, sectoral maturation, and postwar economic growth in Brazil: the resource curse thesis. *Economic Geography*, 257-272.

Auty, Richard M. (2001a). The political economy of resource-driven growth. *European Economic Review, 45*(4), 839-846.

Auty, Richard M. (2001b). The political state and the management of mineral rents in capital-surplus economies: Botswana and Saudi Arabia. *Resources Policy, 27*(2), 77-86.

Auty, Richard M. (2001c). *Resource abundance and economic development*: Oxford University Press.

Auty, Richard M. (2007). Natural resources, capital accumulation and the resource curse. *Ecological Economics, 61*(4), 627-634.

Auty, Richard M, & Mikesell, Raymond French. (1998). *Sustainable development in mineral economies*: Oxford University Press.

Baltagi, Badi. (2008). *Econometric analysis of panel data*: Wiley. com.

Barro, Robert J. (1996). Determinants of economic growth: a cross-country empirical study: National Bureau of Economic Research.

Barro, Robert J, & Lee, Jong Wha. (1996). International measures of schooling years and schooling quality. *The American Economic Review, 86*(2), 218-223.

Basedau, Matthias. (2005). Context Matters-Rethinking the Resource Curse in Sub-Saharan Africa. *Global and Area Studies Working Paper*(1).

Bhattacharyya, Sambit, & Hodler, Roland. (2009). Natural Resources, Democracy and Corruption. *Oxford Centre for the Analysis of Resource Rich Economies*.

Bhattacharyya, Sambit, & Hodler, Roland. (2010). Natural resources, democracy and corruption. *European Economic Review, 54*(4), 608-621.

Birdsall, Nancy, Pinckney, Thomas C, & Sabot, RH. (2000). *Natural resources, human capital, and growth*: Carnegie Endowment for International Peace.

Bornhorst, Fabian, Gupta, Sanjeev, & Thornton, John. (2009). Natural resource endowments and the domestic revenue effort. *European Journal of Political Economy, 25*(4), 439-446.

Boschini, Anne D, Pettersson, Jan, & Roine, Jesper. (2007). Resource Curse or Not: A Question of Appropriability*. *The Scandinavian Journal of Economics, 109*(3), 593-617.

Boyce, John R, & Herbert Emery, JC. (2011). Is a negative correlation between resource abundance and growth sufficient evidence that there is a "resource curse"? *Resources Policy, 36*(1), 1-13.

Brander, James A, & Scott Taylor, M. (1997). International trade between consumer and conservationist countries. *Resource and Energy Economics, 19*(4), 267-297.

Bravo-Ortega, Claudio, & De Gregorio, José. (2005). The Relative Richness of the Poor? Natural Resources, Human Capital, and Economic Growth. *Natural Resources, Human Capital, and Economic Growth (January 2005). World Bank Policy Research Working Paper*(3484).

Breusch, Trevor Stanley, & Pagan, Adrian Rodney. (1980). The Lagrange multiplier test and its applications to model specification in econometrics. *The Review of Economic Studies, 47*(1), 239-253.

Brunnschweiler, Christa N. (2008). Cursing the blessings? Natural resource abundance, institutions, and economic growth. *World Development, 36*(3), 399-419.

Brunnschweiler, Christa N, & Bulte, Erwin H. (2008a). Linking natural resources to slow growth and more conflict. *SCIENCE-NEW YORK THEN WASHINGTON-, 320*, 616.

Brunnschweiler, Christa N, & Bulte, Erwin H. (2008b). The resource curse revisited and revised: A tale of paradoxes and red herrings. *Journal of Environmental Economics and Management, 55*(3), 248-264.

Bulte, Erwin, & Damania, Richard. (2008). Resources for sale: corruption, democracy and the natural resource curse. *The BE Journal of Economic Analysis & Policy, 8*(1).

Bulte, Erwin H, Damania, Richard, & Deacon, Robert. (2003). Resource abundance, poverty and development.

Bulte, Erwin H, Damania, Richard, & Deacon, Robert T. (2005). Resource intensity, institutions, and development. *World Development, 33*(7), 1029-1044.

Carmignani, Fabrizio, & Avom, Desire. (2010). The social development effects of primary commodity export dependence. *Ecological Economics, 70*(2), 317-330.

Caselli, Francesco. (2006). Power struggles and the natural resource curse.

Caselli, Francesco, & Cunningham, Tom. (2009). Leader behaviour and the natural resource curse. *Oxford Economic Papers, 61*(4), 628-650.

Cavalcanti, Tiago V de V, Mohaddes, Kamiar, & Raissi, Mehdi. (2011). Growth, development and natural resources: New evidence using a heterogeneous panel analysis. *The Quarterly Review of Economics and Finance, 51*(4), 305-318.

Chichilnisky, Graciela. (1994). North-south trade and the global environment. *American economic review, 84*(4).

Collier, Paul, & Hoeffler, Anke. (2005). Resource rents, governance, and conflict. *Journal of Conflict Resolution, 49*(4), 625-633.

Coxhead, Ian. (2005). International trade and the natural resource 'curse' in Southeast Asia: does China's growth threaten regional development. *The politics and economics of Indonesia's natural resources. Institute of Southeast Asian Studies, Singapore*, 71-91.

Da Cunha Leite, Carlos, & Weidmann, Jens. (2001). Does mother nature corrupt? Natural resources, corruption, and economic growth. *Natural Resources, Corruption, and Economic Growth (June 1999). IMF Working Paper*(99/85).

Dasgupta, Partha S, & Heal, Geoffrey M. (1980). *Economic theory and exhaustible resources*: Cambridge University Press.

Davis, Graham A, & Tilton, John E. (2005). *The resource curse*. Paper presented at the Natural resources forum.

Dietsche, Evelyn. (2007). The quality of institutions: a cure for the 'resource curse'. *July, Centre for Energy, Petroleum and Mineral Law and Policy, University of Dundee, Oxford Policy Institute.*

Dietz, Simon, Neumayer, Eric, & De Soysa, Indra. (2007). Corruption, the resource curse and genuine saving. *Environment and Development Economics, 12*(1), 33-53.

Ding, Ning, & Field, Barry. (2004). Natural resource abundance and economic growth. *U of Massachusetts Amherst Resource Economics Working Paper*(2004-7).

Ding, Ning, & Field, Barry C. (2005). Natural Resource Abundance and Economic Growths. *Land Economics, 81*(4), 496-502.

Dunning, Thad. (2008). *Crude democracy: Natural resource wealth and political regimes*: Cambridge University Press Cambridge.

FAO, Food. (2007). Agriculture Organization of the United Nations. *Land and Water development Division, 2007a, Georeferenced Database on Africa Dams.*

FAO, JOINT, & FOODS, MICROBIOLOGICAL HAZARDS IN. (2004). Food and Agriculture Organization of the United Nations: Rome.

Fengjun, Zhao. (2006). Resource curse: a literature review. *Journal of Chongqing Technological Business University, 16*(1), 8-12.

Gaitan, Beatriz, & Roe, Terry L. (2005). Natural resource abundance and economic growth in a two country model.

Greene, William H. (2003). *Econometric Analysis, 5/e*: Pearson Education India.

Grilli, Enzo R, & Yang, Maw Cheng. (1988). Primary commodity prices, manufactured goods prices, and the terms of trade of developing countries: what the long run shows. *The World Bank Economic Review, 2*(1), 1-47. Gylfason, Thorvaldur. (2000). Resources, agriculture, and economic growth in economies in transition. *Kyklos, 53*(4), 337-361.

Gylfason, Thorvaldur. (2001a). Natural resources, education, and economic development. *European economic review, 45*(4), 847-859.

Gylfason, Thorvaldur. (2001b). Nature, power and growth. *Scottish Journal of Political Economy, 48*(5), 558-588.

Harford, Tim, & Klein, Michael. (2005). Aid and the Resource Curse: How Can Aid Be Designed to Preserve Institutions?

Herbertsson, Tryggvi Thor, Skuladottir, Marta, & Zoega, Gylfi. (2000). Three symptoms and a cure: A contribution to the economics of the Dutch Disease: CEPR Discussion Papers.

Hodler, Roland. (2006). The curse of natural resources in fractionalized countries. *European Economic Review, 50*(6), 1367-1386.

Humphreys, Macartan, Sachs, Jeffrey, & Stiglitz, Joseph E. (2007). *Escaping the resource curse*: Cambridge Univ Press.

Iimi, Atsushi. (2006). Did Botswana escape from the resource curse?

Isham, Jonathan, Woolcock, Michael, Pritchett, Lant, & Busby, Gwen. (2005). The varieties of resource experience: natural resource export structures and the political economy of economic growth. *The World Bank Economic Review, 19*(2), 141-174.

Jun, Xu Kangning Shao. (2006). Natural Resources Abundance and Economic Growth: A Re-examination of the "Resource Curse" Hypothesis [J]. *The Journal of World Economy, 11*, 006.

Kangning, Xu, & Jian, Wang. (2006). An Empirical Study of A Linkage Between Natural Resource Abundance and Economic Development [J]. *Economic Research Journal, 1*, 78-89.

Karl, Terry Lynn. (2005). 2. Understanding the Resource Curse.

Kim, Yong Jin. (1998). Resource Curse, Over-commitment and Human Capital. *Journal of Economic Development, 23*(2).

Kolstad, Ivar. (2009). The resource curse: which institutions matter? *Applied Economics Letters, 16*(4), 439-442.

Kunte, Arundhati, Hamilton, Kirk, Dixon, John, & Clemens, Michael. (1998). *Estimating national wealth: Methodology and results*: Environment Department, World Bank.

Lane, Philip R, & Tornell, Aaron. (1996). Power, growth, and the voracity effect. *Journal of Economic Growth, 1*(2), 213-241.

Langton, Marcia. (2010). The resource curse. *Griffith Review, 28*, 47-63.

Larsen, Erling Røed. (2004). Escaping the resource curse and the Dutch disease? When and why Norway caught up with and forged ahead of its neighbors.

Larsen, Erling Røed. (2006). Escaping the Resource Curse and the Dutch Disease? *American Journal of Economics and Sociology, 65*(3), 605-640.

Leamer, Edward E. (1995). *The Heckscher-Ohlin model in theory and practice*: International Finance Section, Department of Economics, Princeton University.

Lederman, Daniel, Maloney, William F, Dunning, Thad, & Shelton, Cameron A. (2008). In Search of the Missing Resource Curse [with Comments]. *Economia, 9*(1), 1-57.

Lewis, Tracy R. (1982). Sufficient conditions for extracting least cost resource first. *Econometrica: Journal of the Econometric Society*, 1081-1083.

Lewis, Tracy R, & Schmalensee, Richard. (1982). Cartel deception in nonrenewable resource markets. *The Bell Journal of Economics*, 263-271.

LIU, Rui-ming, & BAI, Yong-xiu. (2008). Resource Curse: a Framework of Neo Classical Economics [J]. *Modern Economic Science, 1*, 015.

Magnus, Jan R, Ji, Kan, & Wang, Wendun. (2010). Resource Abundance and Resource Dependence in China.

Manning, Alexis. (2004). Human Capital as a Transmission Mechanism of the Resource Curse. *The Park Place Economist, 12*, 75-86.

Manzano, Osmel, & Rigobon, Roberto. (2001). Resource curse or debt overhang? : National Bureau of Economic Research.

Martin, Sala I. X. y A. Subramanian (2003), "Addressing the Natural Resource Curse: An Illustration from Nigeria". *NBER working paper*(9804).

Matsuyama, Kiminori. (1992). Agricultural productivity, comparative advantage, and economic growth. *Journal of economic theory, 58*(2), 317-334.

Mehlum, Halvor, Moene, Kalle, & Torvik, Ragnar. (2002). Institutions and the resource curse.

Mehlum, Halvor, Moene, Karl, & Torvik, Ragnar. (2006a). Cursed by resources or institutions? *The World Economy, 29*(8), 1117-1131.

Mehlum, Halvor, Moene, Karl, & Torvik, Ragnar. (2006b). Institutions and the Resource Curse*. *The Economic Journal, 116*(508), 1-20.

Murshed, Syed Mansoob. (2004). When does natural resource abundance lead to a resource curse? : International Institute for Environment and Development, Environmental Economics Programme.

Neary, J Peter, & Van Wijnbergen, Sweder. (1986). Natural resources and the macroeconomy.

Norman, Catherine S. (2009). Rule of law and the resource curse: abundance versus intensity. *Environmental and Resource Economics, 43*(2), 183-207.

North, Douglass C. (1990). *Institutions, institutional change and economic performance*: Cambridge university press.

Papyrakis, Elissaios, & Gerlagh, Reyer. (2004). The resource curse hypothesis and its transmission channels. *Journal of Comparative Economics, 32*(1), 181-193.

Papyrakis, Elissaios, & Gerlagh, Reyer. (2007). Resource abundance and economic growth in the United States. *European Economic Review, 51*(4), 1011-1039.

Polterovich, Victor, & Popov, Vladimir. (2007). Democratization, quality of institutions and economic growth. *Quality of Institutions and Economic Growth (July 2007)*.

Polterovich, Victor, Popov, Vladimir, & Tonis, Alexander. (2010). Resource abundance: A curse or blessing?

Rabe-Hesketh, Sophia, & Skrondal, Anders. (2008). *Multilevel and longitudinal modelling using Stata*: STATA press.

Ramsey, Frank Plumpton. (1928). A mathematical theory of saving. *The Economic Journal, 38*(152), 543-559.

Robinson, James A, Torvik, Ragnar, & Verdier, Thierry. (2006). Political foundations of the resource curse. *Journal of development Economics, 79*(2), 447-468.

Ross, Michael L. (2003). The natural resource curse: How wealth can make you poor. *Natural resources and violent conflict: options and actions*, 17-42.

Sachs, Jeffrey D, & Warner, Andrew M. (1995). Natural resource abundance and economic growth: National Bureau of Economic Research.

Sachs, Jeffrey D, & Warner, Andrew M. (1997). Sources of slow growth in African economies. *Journal of African economies, 6*(3), 335-376.

Sachs, Jeffrey D, & Warner, Andrew M. (1999). The big push, natural resource booms and growth. *Journal of development economics, 59*(1), 43-76.

Sachs, Jeffrey D, & Warner, Andrew M. (2001). The curse of natural resources. *European economic review, 45*(4), 827-838.

Sala-i-Martin, Xavier. (2006). The world distribution of income: falling poverty and... convergence, period. *The Quarterly Journal of Economics, 121*(2), 351-397.

Sandbu, Martin E. (2006). Natural wealth accounts: A proposal for alleviating the natural resource curse. *World Development, 34*(7), 1153-1170.

Sarraf, Maria, & Jiwanji, Moortaza. (2001). Beating the resource curse. *The case of Botswana, Environment Department, World Bank, Washington DC.*

Shaxson, Nicholas. (2007). Oil, corruption and the resource curse. *International Affairs, 83*(6), 1123-1140.

Siddiqui, Masood, & Adnan Hye, Qazi. (2010). Economic growth and management of natural resources in the case of Pakistan. *European Journal of Economics, Finance and Administrative Sciences*(22).

Siegle, Joseph. (2005). Governance strategies to remedy the natural resource curse. *International Social Science Journal, 57*(s1), 45-55.

Snyder, Richard, & Bhavnani, Ravi. (2005). Diamonds, Blood, and Taxes A Revenue-Centered Framework for Explaining Political Order. *Journal of Conflict Resolution, 49*(4), 563-597.

Solow, Robert M. (1956). A contribution to the theory of economic growth. *The quarterly journal of economics, 70*(1), 65-94.

Stevens, Paul. (2003). Resource Impact-Curse or Blessing? *Investment Policy, 22*, 5.6.

Stevens, Paul, & Dietsche, Evelyn. (2008). Resource curse: An analysis of causes, experiences and possible ways forward. *Energy Policy, 36*(1), 56-65.

Stiglitz, Joseph E. (2005). Making Natural Resources into a Blessing rather than a Curse. *Covering Oil. A Reporter's Guide to Energy and Development*.

Stijns, Jean-Philippe. (2006). Natural resource abundance and human capital accumulation. *World Development, 34*(6), 1060-1083.

Stijns, Jean-Philippe C. (2005). Natural resource abundance and economic growth revisited. *Resources policy, 30*(2), 107-130.

Suslova, Elena, & Volchkova, Natalya. (2007). Human capital, industrial growth, and resource curse. *CEFIR WP.*

Swan, Trevor W. (1956). Economic growth and capital accumulation. *Economic record, 32*(2), 334-361.

Tornell, Aaron, & Lane, Philip R. (1998). Are windfalls a curse?: a non-representative agent model of the current account. *Journal of International Economics, 44*(1), 83-112.

Torvik, Ragnar. (2009). Why do some resource-abundant countries succeed while others do not? *Oxford Review of Economic Policy, 25*(2), 241-256.

Van der Ploeg, Frederick, & Poelhekke, Steven. (2009). Volatility and the natural resource curse. *Oxford economic papers, 61*(4), 727-760.

Wenar, Leif. (2008). Property rights and the resource curse. *Philosophy & Public Affairs, 36*(1), 2-32.

Wick, Katharina, & Bulte, Erwin. (2009). The curse of natural resources. *Annu. Rev. Resour. Econ., 1*(1), 139-156.

Wick, Katharina, & Bulte, Erwin H. (2006). Contesting resources–rent seeking, conflict and the natural resource curse. *Public Choice, 128*(3-4), 457-476.

Wick, Katharina, & Bulte, Erwin H. (2006). Rent Seeking, Conflict and the Natural Resource Curse. *Springer: Public Choice, Vol. 128, No. 3/4,* 457-476.

Wooldridge, Jeffrey M. (2002). *Econometric Analysis of cross-section and panel data*: The MIT Press. Cambridge, Massachusetts, London, England.

Wright, Gavin, & Czelusta, Jesse. (2004). Why economies slow: the myth of the resource curse. *Challenge, 47*(2), 6-38.

Appendix

Table 5.3 Total Natural Resource rent and Economic Growth

	(1) GDP per capita Growth	(2) GDP per capita growth	(3) GDP per capita growth	(4) GDP per capita growth	(5) GDP per capita growth	(6) GDP per capita growth	(7) GDP per capita growth
Total natural resource rent	0.0915***	0.1035***	0.1918***	0.2077***	0.1732***	0.1748***	0.1719***
	(0.0152)	(0.0150)	(0.0184)	(0.0189)	(0.0225)	(0.0222)	(0.0303)
Initial income		-4.5610***	-4.0949***	-4.7933***	-3.1740***	-4.4557***	-4.1183***
		(0.5337)	(0.5453)	(0.5625)	(0.6849)	(0.7096)	(0.7705)
Education			0.0466***	0.0377***	0.0489***	0.0442***	0.0471***
			(0.0100)	(0.0106)	(0.0107)	(0.0106)	(0.0107)
Investment				0.1862***	0.1906***	0.1752***	0.1349***
				(0.0196)	(0.0230)	(0.0229)	(0.0254)
Corruption					-0.8750***	-0.7909***	-0.7519***
					(0.1342)	(0.1335)	(0.1579)
Openness						0.0018***	0.0008*
						(0.0003)	(0.0003)
Terms of Trade							-0.0008
							(0.0056)
_cons	1.2312***	36.1917***	27.3500***	29.6648***	20.0836***	28.7321***	26.5702***
	(0.1501)	(4.0942)	(4.0811)	(4.2003)	(5.4647)	(5.5901)	(5.7921)
N	3571	3535	2783	2592	1793	1793	1416
R^2	0.111	0.130	0.176	0.210	0.331	0.346	0.426

Table 5.5 Regional Analysis of Total Natural Resource rents and Economic Growth

	(1) GDP per capita growth	(2) GDP per capita growth	(3) GDP per capita growth	(4) GDP per capita growth	(5) GDP per capita growth	(6) GDP per capita growth	(7) GDP per capita growth
Initial income	-4.1841***	-4.1087***	-4.5006***	-4.1273***	-4.0537***	-4.0907***	-4.2965***
	(0.7697)	(0.7715)	(0.7750)	(0.7699)	(0.7702)	(0.7711)	(0.7790)
Education	0.0475***	0.0473***	0.0495***	0.0483***	0.0483***	0.0470***	0.0479***
	(0.0107)	(0.0107)	(0.0107)	(0.0107)	(0.0107)	(0.0107)	(0.0107)
Investment	0.1321***	0.1352***	0.1382***	0.1345***	0.1345***	0.1352***	0.1366***
	(0.0254)	(0.0254)	(0.0253)	(0.0254)	(0.0254)	(0.0254)	(0.0254)
Corruption	-0.7590***	-0.7508***	-0.7716***	-0.7476***	-0.7665***	-0.7479***	-0.7440***
	(0.1577)	(0.1580)	(0.1573)	(0.1578)	(0.1579)	(0.1580)	(0.1579)
Openness	0.0008*	0.0008*	0.0010**	0.0008*	0.0007*	0.0008*	0.0009**
	(0.0003)	(0.0003)	(0.0003)	(0.0003)	(0.0003)	(0.0003)	(0.0003)
Terms of Trade	0.0007	-0.0010	0.0013	-0.0001	0.0006	-0.0008	-0.0007
	(0.0057)	(0.0057)	(0.0056)	(0.0057)	(0.0057)	(0.0056)	(0.0056)
Total natural resource rent	0.1802***	0.1729***	0.1282***	0.1421***	0.1941***	0.1726***	0.1963***
	(0.0305)	(0.0305)	(0.0327)	(0.0349)	(0.0321)	(0.0303)	(0.0343)
South Asia	-0.2781*						
	(0.1186)						
North America		-0.1229					
		(0.4205)					
Middle East and North Africa			0.2387***				
			(0.0684)				
Europe and Central Asia				0.0938			
				(0.0545)			
Sub Saharan Africa					-0.1265*		
					(0.0612)		
Latin America and Caribbean						-0.8034	
						(0.8414)	
East Asia and Pacific							-0.0855
							(0.0562)
_cons	27.0119***	26.4941***	28.7828***	26.5970***	25.9699***	26.3826***	27.7305***
	(5.7851)	(5.8001)	(5.8018)	(5.7877)	(5.7921)	(5.7957)	(5.8392)
N	1416	1416	1416	1416	1416	1416	1416
R²	0.428	0.426	0.431	0.427	0.428	0.426	0.427

Standard errors in parentheses
* $p < 0.05$, ** $p < 0.01$, *** $p < 0.001$

Table 5.6 Regional Anaysis of Oil rents and Economic Growth

	(1) GDP per capita growth	(2) GDP per capita growth	(3) GDP per capita growth	(4) GDP per capita growth	(5) GDP per capita growth	(6) GDP per capita growth	(7) GDP per capita growth
Initial income	-3.9060***	-3.8232***	-4.7827***	-3.8086***	-3.7317***	-3.8113***	-4.1587***
	(0.7453)	(0.7500)	(0.7496)	(0.7457)	(0.7447)	(0.7461)	(0.7535)
Education	0.0364**	0.0362**	0.0385**	0.0359**	0.0387**	0.0356**	0.0341**
	(0.0130)	(0.0131)	(0.0128)	(0.0130)	(0.0130)	(0.0130)	(0.0130)
Investment	0.1741***	0.1773***	0.1992***	0.1744***	0.1783***	0.1776***	0.1803***
	(0.0278)	(0.0279)	(0.0276)	(0.0278)	(0.0277)	(0.0278)	(0.0278)
Corruption	-0.6451***	-0.6408***	-0.7377***	-0.6302***	-0.6375***	-0.6397***	-0.6574***
	(0.1566)	(0.1569)	(0.1551)	(0.1569)	(0.1563)	(0.1568)	(0.1565)
Openness	0.0015***	0.0015***	0.0016***	0.0015***	0.0013***	0.0015***	0.0016***
	(0.0004)	(0.0004)	(0.0003)	(0.0004)	(0.0004)	(0.0004)	(0.0004)
Terms of trade	-0.0001	-0.0018	0.0009	-0.0013	0.0006	-0.0016	-0.0027
	(0.0053)	(0.0053)	(0.0052)	(0.0053)	(0.0053)	(0.0053)	(0.0053)
Oil rent	0.2691***	0.2628***	0.1683***	0.2304***	0.3076***	0.2630***	0.3360***
	(0.0407)	(0.0407)	(0.0428)	(0.0453)	(0.0436)	(0.0406)	(0.0496)
South Asia	-0.3898*						
	(0.1924)						
North America		-0.6921					
		(2.1204)					
Middle East and North Africa			0.6054***				
			(0.0987)				
Europe and Central Asia				0.1278			
				(0.0817)			
Sub Saharan Africa					-0.2398**		
					(0.0853)		
Latin America and Caribbean						-1.8846	
						(1.4264)	
East Asia and Pacific							-0.1908**
							(0.0737)
_cons	24.8829***	24.2966***	30.8698***	24.2703***	23.4143***	24.2578***	26.9394***
	(5.7647)	(5.8128)	(5.7719)	(5.7683)	(5.7657)	(5.7713)	(5.8305)
N	1243	1243	1243	1243	1243	1243	1243
R^2	0.476	0.474	0.491	0.475	0.477	0.474	0.477

Standard errors in parentheses
* $p < 0.05$, ** $p < 0.01$, *** $p < 0.001$

Table 5.7 Sample of top 40 oil reserve countries

	(1) GDP per capita growth	(2) GDP per capita growth	(3) GDP per capita growth
Initial income	-6.4263*** (1.3152)	-6.4588*** (1.3318)	-7.1396*** (1.3504)
Education	0.0253 (0.0335)	0.0338 (0.0341)	0.0137 (0.0345)
Investment	0.3075*** (0.0586)	0.3026*** (0.0593)	0.2566*** (0.0608)
Corruption	-0.3353 (0.3491)	-0.4560 (0.3519)	-0.4970 (0.3572)
Openness	0.0115*** (0.0030)	0.0130*** (0.0030)	0.0118*** (0.0032)
Terms of trade	-0.0005 (0.0082)	0.0034 (0.0084)	0.0187** (0.0067)
Total natural resource rents	0.1675*** (0.0382)		
Oil rents		0.1836*** (0.0520)	
Mineral rents			0.3489* (0.1676)
_cons	38.4332*** (11.2352)	38.0856*** (11.4210)	48.0453*** (11.5889)
N	314	314	314
R^2	0.575	0.565	0.553

Standard errors in parentheses
* $p < 0.05$, ** $p < 0.01$, *** $p < 0.001$

Table 5.8 Oil rents and Economic Growth- at different income group level and interaction of corruption

	(1) GDP per capita Growth	(2) GDP per capita Growth	(3) GDP per capita Growth	(4) GDP per capita Growth	(5) GDP per capita Growth	(6) GDP per Capita Growth
Initial Income	-3.7140***	-3.8376***	-3.7801***	-3.8369***	-3.7338***	-4.1024***
	(0.7453)	(0.7456)	(0.7473)	(0.7463)	(0.7456)	(0.7837)
Education	0.0387**	0.0356**	0.0353**	0.0353**	0.0352**	0.0453***
	(0.0130)	(0.0130)	(0.0130)	(0.0131)	(0.0130)	(0.0109)
Investment	0.1772***	0.1776***	0.1742***	0.1764***	0.1768***	0.1090***
	(0.0277)	(0.0278)	(0.0279)	(0.0278)	(0.0277)	(0.0256)
Corruption	-0.6173***	-0.6408***	-0.6527***	-0.6376***	-0.5934***	-0.6982***
	(0.1566)	(0.1568)	(0.1569)	(0.1571)	(0.1577)	(0.1639)
Openness	0.0012***	0.0015***	0.0015***	0.0015***	0.0015***	0.0012***
	(0.0004)	(0.0004)	(0.0004)	(0.0004)	(0.0004)	(0.0003)
Terms of Trade	0.0001	-0.0014	-0.0017	-0.0022	-0.0033	0.0115*
	(0.0053)	(0.0053)	(0.0053)	(0.0054)	(0.0053)	(0.0050)
Oil rent	0.2931***	0.2638***	0.2550***	0.2887***	0.2232***	
	(0.0421)	(0.0406)	(0.0409)	(0.0650)	(0.0435)	
High Income Non-OECD	-0.2994**					
	(0.1092)					
High Income OECD		-0.7326				
		(0.5787)				
Low Income			0.3348			
			(0.2544)			
Lower Middle Income				-0.0389		
				(0.0740)		
Upper Middle income					0.2075*	
					(0.0843)	
Mineral rent						0.5480***
						(0.1216)
Mineral*Corruption						-0.1346***
						(0.0405)
_cons	23.3246***	24.5024***	24.1152***	24.4583***	23.6059***	26.4464***
	(5.7698)	(5.7683)	(5.7762)	(5.7729)	(5.7689)	(5.9602)
N	1243	1243	1243	1243	1243	1416
R^2	0.477	0.474	0.474	0.474	0.476	0.421

Standard errors in parentheses
* $p < 0.05$, ** $p < 0.01$, *** $p < 0.001$

Table 5.9 Total Natural resource rents and economic growth at different Income group level

	(1) GDP capita growth	(2) GDP capita growth	(3) GDP capita growth	(4) GDP capita growth	(5) GDP capita growth	(6) GDP capita growth	(7) GDP capita growth
Initial income	-4.0862***	-4.1030***	-4.1976***	-4.1164***	-4.1431***	-4.0616***	-4.4690***
	(0.7696)	(0.7704)	(0.7741)	(0.7714)	(0.7691)	(0.7762)	(0.7487)
Education	0.0484***	0.0470***	0.0484***	0.0470***	0.0471***	0.0476***	0.0351**
	(0.0107)	(0.0107)	(0.0108)	(0.0108)	(0.0107)	(0.0107)	(0.0129)
Investment	0.1342***	0.1359***	0.1367***	0.1349***	0.1373***	0.1333***	0.1920***
	(0.0254)	(0.0254)	(0.0255)	(0.0254)	(0.0254)	(0.0255)	(0.0277)
Corruption	-0.7396***	-0.7512***	-0.7332***	-0.7521***	-0.7216***	-0.7526***	-0.6674***
	(0.1578)	(0.1579)	(0.1589)	(0.1580)	(0.1581)	(0.1580)	(0.1553)
Openness	0.0007*	0.0008*	0.0008*	0.0008*	0.0008*	0.0008*	0.0015***
	(0.0003)	(0.0003)	(0.0003)	(0.0003)	(0.0003)	(0.0003)	(0.0004)
Terms of Trade	0.0006	-0.0002	-0.0007	-0.0009	-0.0020	-0.0004	0.0003
	(0.0057)	(0.0057)	(0.0056)	(0.0057)	(0.0057)	(0.0057)	(0.0052)
Total natural resource rent	0.1850***	0.1726***	0.1823***	0.1737***	0.1399***	0.1822***	
	(0.0309)	(0.0303)	(0.0319)	(0.0417)	(0.0330)	(0.0346)	
High Income Non-OECD	-0.1867*						
	(0.0879)						
High Income OECD		-0.3956					
		(0.3152)					
Low income			-0.0801				
			(0.0760)				
Lower Middle income				-0.0032			
				(0.0505)			
Upper Middle income					0.1381*		
					(0.0565)		
Muslims						-0.0325	
						(0.0528)	
Oil rents							0.6568***
							(0.0894)
_cons	26.2705***	26.4723***	26.9403***	26.5654***	26.7375***	26.1440***	28.9817***
	(5.7860)	(5.7914)	(5.8025)	(5.7949)	(5.7814)	(5.8347)	(5.7816)
N	1416	1416	1416	1416	1416	1416	1243
R^2	0.428	0.427	0.426	0.426	0.429	0.426	0.485

Standard errors in parentheses
* $p < 0.05$, ** $p < 0.01$, *** $p < 0.001$

Graphs,

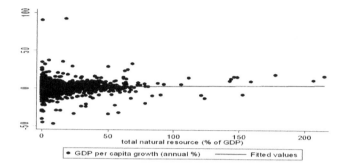

Figure 5.1

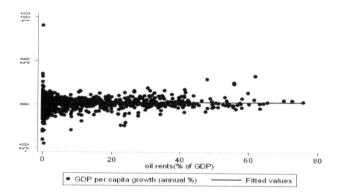

Figure 5.2.

58

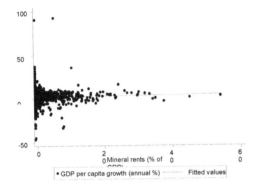

Figure 5.33

Lightning Source UK Ltd.
Milton Keynes UK
UKOW05f0623190617

303652UK00001B/138/P